Praise for

"*Story of My People* conveys the e ... was fun...Mr. Nesi's musings are as finely woven as his textiles."
—*New York Times*

"In this blend of memoir, manifesto, and diatribe, [Nesi] gives an intimate account of a homespun world, 'glistening and weightless like silk,' destroyed by civilization...In gleefully biting prose, Nesi excoriates Italy's politicians, its arrogant economists, and the 'titanic foreign multinationals' who 'sell their heartless, unimaginative rags, and *shmattes* everywhere around the world.'" —*The New Yorker*

"This unique book—part memoir, part argument for the reformation of the global financial system—tumbles out of itself on the page, and reading it was an equally propulsive experience. It rhapsodizes and slaps its chest in true Italian style, makes frequent allusions with a disarming bluntness (to Machiavelli, to Richard Ford, to Paul Newman movies), and always has something to say. I finished and instantly went back to reread certain pages."
—John Jeremiah Sullivan, author of *Pulphead*

"Who would have thought that memoir and polemic could work together so well? A totally absorbing story, and a portrait of modern Italy." — Sarah Bakewell, National Book Critics Circle Award—winning author of *How to Live*

"A searing indictment of globalization's failures, and the inability of politicians and pundits to consider its impact on real lives...much of the book is sad, honest, and biting; overall it is an important work."
—*Publishers Weekly*

"At once a memoir, a requiem, and a work of social and literary criticism about the toll this shift took on his city and psyche...fiercely angry, conflicted, and often beautifully written." —*Bookforum*

"This is probably one of my favorite books of the year, period, nonfiction or no." —*Bookavore*

"[T]he single best book about globalization...in a long time. [*Story of My People*] takes the abstract implications of globalization and reduces it to a very personal level." —*Publishing Perspectives*

"*Story of My People* is one of those knockout punches that literature throws at the world every now and then."
—Sandro Veronesi, Strega Prize–winning author

"*Story of My People* is a well-told story but also an eloquent and pained wail about loss. Globalization has swallowed up the artisans, the families, and the beautiful fabrics at the heart of Prato's weaving industry, and a world has unraveled like a skein of yarn. While Nesi clearly understands the economics and even the inevitability of this transition for Italy's family manufacturers, he will not let this world disappear without describing it for the rest of us. A business and family can do everything right and still have everything go wrong. This is an important, poetic, and personal work of industrial history."
—Pietra Rivoli, author of *The Travels of a T-shirt in the Global Economy*

"A remarkable evocation of the vanished world of artisan capitalism in Tuscany, swept away by hurricane globalization. 'Why should this destruction be?' asks the author and former owner of a small family textile business, in a mingled cry of pain and anger."
—Robert Skidelsky, author of *How Much Is Enough?*

"A tour de force that spares no one." —*Kirkus*

"Few have produced an account of globalization's effects as personal, poignant, and beautifully written as Edoardo Nesi's *Story of My People*."
—*New York Journal of Books*

"Thought provoking and beautifully written, and also heartbreaking...whether or not you agree with [Nesi's] point of view, the book will make you think." —*Hudson Valley News*

"...now we have another classic by someone on the wrong end of history...The story of Prato's demise is lyrically written and deeply moving...It is impossible to read this book without feeling that something must be done." —*Finance & Development*

"...an eloquent, angry, exquisitely written little book. A combination of memoir and cultural commentary."
—Emily St. John Mandel, author of *The Lola Quartet* and *Last Night in Montreal*

"An eloquent, emotion-laden, and, I think, essential addition to the globalization bookshelf…If I were a publisher, this is a book I'd be proud to put out." —*strategy+business*

"From the 1950s to the 1980s, much of Italy was a charmed place, its beauty wreathed in wealth. Edoardo Nesi's gracefully nostalgic memoir, *Story of My People*, is of that time…You feel saddened for the narrator and his family, and what they have lost. You feel saddened *with* him too, as you recognize in yourself something of the same regret for a world—not just an Italian one—that is passing. The fact that this regret is thickly gilded with sentiment makes it no less poignant. Edoardo Nesi has mined his own memories, and thus touches ours." —*Financial Times*

"[This] is no ordinary of account of a country's industrial collapse. The brilliance of this depressing story (winner of Italy's Strega Prize) is Edoardo Nesi's imaginative fusion of history and autobiography, infused with vignettes of the lives of individual workers who have suffered. Yes, this is also the author's account of how he became a successful writer. But most of all it is the depiction of an era that is just about over, at the end of its collapse." —*CounterPunch*

"[*Story of My People*] has the driving force of a polemic but the wisdom of a novel, and is the only book about the global recession I'd recommend to anybody, though you need have no interest in the economy to pick it up. It is one of the best books I've read all year without question." —*Library Reads*

"…Nesi forms a sharp and timely indictment of runaway globalization, fast fashion, and big business." —*Blouin Artinfo*

"[Nesi's] heartbreaking narrative describes a struggling country that is just as fascinating and rich as the Italy advertised through the tourism industry, and much more real." —*TriQuarterly*

"[A]n unfamiliar mix of memoir and the politics of business…worth reading for anyone who likes good writing and wants a deeper understanding of either contemporary Europe or global business." —*Book News*

"[Nesi] chronicles the sad story of free trade's impact on 'his people' in the town of Prato, capturing the distinctive pain of a modern European left behind, a cultural stranger in his own land." —*Foreign Affairs*

STORY

of

MY PEOPLE

Edoardo Nesi

translated from the Italian by Antony Shugaar

OTHER PRESS
NEW YORK

Copyright © RCS Libri S.p.A.—Milano, Bompiani 2010
Originally published as *Storia della mia gente* by Bompiani

Translation copyright © 2012 Antony Shugaar

First softcover edition 2014
ISBN 978-1-59051-677-5

Epigraph taken from *Some Sort of Epic Grandeur: The Life of F. Scott Fitzgerald*, by Matthew J.
Bruccoli (Columbia: University of South Carolina Press, 2002).

Production Editor: Yvonne E. Cárdenas
Text Designer: Jennifer Daddio/Bookmark Design & Media, Inc.
This book was set in 12.5 pt Centaur MT
by Alpha Design & Composition of Pittsfield, NH

1 3 5 9 10 8 6 4 2

Library of Congress Cataloging-in-Publication Data

Nesi, Edoardo, 1964–
[Storia della mia gente. English]
Story of My People / by Edoardo Nesi ; translated into English by Antony Shugaar.
pages cm
ISBN 978-1-59051-554-9 (hardcover) — ISBN (invalid) 978-1-59051-555-6 (ebook)
1. Lanificio T.O. Nesi & figli—History.   2. Textile industry—Italy—Prato.
3. Nesi, Edoardo, 1964–   4. Businessmen—Italy—Prato—Biography.   I. Shugaar,
Antony, translator.   II. Title.
HD9905.I74L36713 2013
338.7'6670092—dc23
[B]
2012039787

Ettore

and

Angelica

It is the most beautiful history in the world.
It is the history of me and of my people.

—F. SCOTT FITZGERALD

The Lanificio T.O. Nesi
& Figli S.p.A.

In September 2004—on September 7, 2004—I sold my family's textile company.

First established as a weaving mill in the 1920s, the company shifted operations right after World War II, becoming a woolen mill with the somewhat portentous name of Lanificio T.O. Nesi & Figli S.p.A. Looking down over my shoulder as I write is a framed enlargement of a black-and-white photograph of the weaving mill, dated 1926. There are three gigantic looms surrounded by men, women, and children, all staring into the camera lens. To one side, with a grim look in his eye and his hat perched at a rakish angle, stands my grandfather, Temistocle Nesi. At the leftmost edge of the picture, dressed in a white shirt, a vest, and abundant, loose-fitting trousers, and a good fifteen years older, is Omero Nesi, Temistocle's brother. The two of them were the founding partners—the reason why the company is named T.O. Nesi & Figli. Temistocle Omero Nesi & Figli—Themistocles Homer Nesi & Sons.

We never did find out why their parents—who bore the rather common names of Adamo and Maria—chose to give their sons, born in the twilight years of the nineteenth century, such unlikely names, befitting Greek heroes. Still, names are the first gift that a parent bestows upon a child, and I still wonder whether they even knew (neither of them had finished elementary school) that they had named one son after the supreme blind poet, and the other son after a general who was the last great hero of the Athenian republic. In other words, did they know that they had intertwined in the names of their newborn sons the force of arms and the power of letters?—as if they sensed that even a name might become an important tool in a weaver's life in the early years of the new century in Narnali, a village that snuggled around its church, at the head of the ancient road that runs from Prato to Pistoia.

Seated on a wooden crate full of white yarn, the distinctive whitish hue of greasy wool, dressed in shorts and with an elfin gleam in his eyes, is Omero's son Alfiero. He might be ten, or even twelve. He's a child. Still, in the minds of the two founding partners, the company as a whole is designed around him. From the outset, they meant for the Lanificio T.O. Nesi & Figli to weather the years, to exist long after the founders had left this mortal coil, and they certainly meant for Alfiero to lead the company, a company that was founded for the future more than the present, for the children who had already come into the world and those yet to come.

Alvarado, who was Temistocle's son and my father, was born six years after that picture was taken, in 1932, weighing in at almost thirteen pounds. He was the second son born to Temistocle and Rosa, and he was conceived in the immediate aftermath of the first Alvarado's death. The first Alvarado had also come into the world with the sheer weight of a colossus and had died one night in his crib; his parents took him into their bed and watched over him until dawn in an impromptu wake. My father also came into this world with his fate already decided: the company lay in his future, whether he liked it or not, and while the Spanish origin of his name is immediately apparent, we never knew why Temistocle gave him that name—and, as if that weren't enough, also saddled him with the middle name Gualberto. The one time I visited Los Angeles, I took a picture of the street sign at the corner of Alvarado Street and later showed it to him. He looked at it for a few seconds, then turned to me and said only, "I can't think of a thing to say."

I was born in 1964 and, while I have a far more commonplace first name than seems to be the rule in my family,

I carry my grandfather's first name as my middle name. Together with my brothers Federico and Lorenzo, I'm a member of what was meant to be the third textiles-manufacturing generation of the Nesi family—and I'd been promised the world.

It was never stated in so many words—in fact I can't imagine anything that my father would have been more unlikely to do—but the very state of things conveyed the idea clearly. My upbringing practically shouted it out loud. The world was at my disposal. If I only had the skill, the courage, and the strength of will, I'd be successful. There were no limits to what I could do, except limits I set for myself. If I wanted to spend a summer studying in America, for instance, I had only to say the word. So when I did say the word, at age fifteen in the summer of 1979, after a long winter spent listening to songs by Bob Dylan and Neil Young, I promptly flew to California to study English at UC Berkeley. Alone.

My indelible memory of those days is of a campus overrun by a herd of aging boys in wheelchairs, all Vietnam vets. They weren't enrolled in classes, or maybe they just weren't enrolled anymore, but they were always there, wandering the campus. At night they drank and got rowdy, but no one said a thing. The one who made the most ruckus always wore a fantastic threadbare hussar's dress cavalry jacket, and had a long beard and an impressive girlfriend. We always said hello.

When I informed my professors that I wouldn't be attending English classes because I already spoke English well, they told me that they understood—after all, it was July 1979, at *Berkeley*. They just told me to sign a form, and from that day on all I did was ride up and down the dizzying hillsides of San Francisco aboard the clattering little cable cars they have there, the Golden Gate Bridge filling my eyes and the wind off the Pacific buffeting my face, constantly astonished by everything I saw. I remember wondering frequently how the people in that city managed to support themselves, without working in the textile industry. Where did they get their money? Who supported them, if they didn't even have so much as a spinning mill, a yarn-twisting plant, or a wool-carbonizing facility?

After that, I spent many summers in America, doing my best to escape Prato and my predestined fate, making a special effort to attend the summer sessions of their finest universities. I was proud to find myself for the first time in my life in a place where everyone you met was there because they'd passed through a selection process. Sure, even though the summer sessions were at best distant relations of the winter sessions, and in practical terms all you had to do was pay your fee and you were accepted, at the age of eighteen it's a tough thing to spend your summers shut up in a library, studying both the History of International Relations and Mergers & Acquisitions.

Alone again, I spent the summer of 1982 at Cornell, with its wonderful campus set in the forests of upstate New York, and it was there that I watched Italy's victory in the World Cup Finals one morning, eager and anxious, surrounded and encouraged by a group of the offspring of Lebanese political refugees. It was not until many years later that I learned that Cornell was where Thomas Pynchon and Richard Fariña had studied—the whole time he was there, Pynchon ardently wished he could be Fariña, while Fariña wrote short stories that were regularly published by literary journals. Fariña was the most admired young man on campus until he was expelled, trailing clouds of glory, for organizing a student demonstration. His course set, he threw himself headlong into the dizzy whirl of life in the incredible America of those years, becoming a friend of Bob Dylan's and marrying the barely seventeen-year-old Mimi Baez, Joan Baez's sister, and starting a folk duo that debuted in 1964 at the Big Sur Folk Festival. Even as he seemed on track to become a great protest singer and songwriter, he kept working on his novel, *Been Down So Long It Looks Like Up to Me* (which, when I became the editorial director of Fandango Libri for a few weeks, I had translated into Italian, proudly publishing it under the title *Così giù che mi sembra di star su*), only to be killed, just two days after the novel's publication, in a motorcycle crash outside of Carmel—Richard Fariña, in 1966, dead at age twenty-nine.

I attended not one but two summer sessions at Harvard. As I forced myself to study and play with the blind resolve of pure ambition, drifting off into reveries of ivy-covered universities, daydreams that always culminated in my graduation ceremony in Harvard Yard, with my parents tearing up and the mortarboards tossed into the air and the orchestra playing "Auld Lang Syne," I spent my days in the throes of spells of lassitude and homesickness like any emigrant, and by night various Italian stragglers and I would let ourselves be driven around by a pizza maker from Abruzzo in his forties who had a Jaguar. He would cruise slowly through the streets of Boston with the air-conditioning cranked to the highest setting, chain-smoking and talking constantly and obsessively about how much he missed Italy, just like me. I couldn't help but feel like a voluntary prisoner of the world's most beautiful college campus, and I desired nothing so much as the dawning of the day when I could finally return home, and in fact every night when the sun set, I'd scratch a tally mark on my dorm room wall, just like a convict in a prison cell.

In what I thought of as late afternoon, after a dinner that according to incomprehensible Saxon custom started at five and ended at six, I would sit on the steps outside Widener Library, the enormous neoclassical pile in which I'd fallen asleep so many times, with my head resting on a copy of Machiavelli's *The Prince*. I'd start imagining my friends back home who, taking advantage of the fact that they were six hours ahead of me and possessed priorities that were radically different from the ones I had imposed upon myself, were about to walk into La Capannina, the seaside nightclub at Forte dei Marmi. I dreamed of going there myself some Saturday night, by taking advantage of those super-discounted airline tickets touted by the travel agencies that sprang up like weeds all around campus, with special deals that promised to deliver me to Rome airport early Saturday morning, giving me all the time I needed to travel north to Forte dei Marmi where I could tell one very special young girl two or three important facts—without a wink of sleep because when you're young, there really is no need to sleep—and then take off again from Rome on Sunday morning, getting into Boston fresh as a daisy later that afternoon, ready for a full day of lessons on Monday.

When I returned home from Harvard—where thanks to my own lack of determination and a cunning game of defense played by my parents I never did muster the courage to enroll in the winter semesters, the hard sessions, the real ones—I washed up on the shores of an unsuccessful experience at the University of Florence, School of Law, a career prospect that I embraced recklessly in the wake of my surge of enthusiasm for a movie that was popular at the time, *The Verdict.*

On the first day of classes, I already knew I wasn't cut out for it.

In a huge lecture hall packed wall to wall with young boys and girls just like me—packed so full that I couldn't even get through the door—Professor Aldo Schiavone was teaching a class on Roman law. I was forced to retreat to the lecture hall next door, similarly jam-packed, where it was difficult to see and almost impossible to hear Professor Schiavone as he lectured on Numa Pompilio from a television monitor, without managing to convey the masterful authority that he—perhaps—emanated in the flesh. There was a tremendous din in the hall and I could barely make out every other word, and everyone was smoking, and I immediately understood that attending lectures would only be a waste of my time, and that I'd never be able to study whole books at a time all by myself, alone, at home, with no one else to talk to. I had fucked up completely. I'd shoehorned myself into a course of study where I was expected to do the one thing I'd never been good at, that is, memorizing dozens and dozens of concepts, all of equal importance.

After passing five final oral exams in the first year, including one on private law, I flunked the *written* exam on public law not once but twice, and I retreated, my tail between my legs. My mother was disappointed, heartbroken really. Not my father. He couldn't wait for me to start work in the textile company, and he told me that he'd always secretly feared that if I became a lawyer, I would become impossibly arrogant.

Cursus Honorum

So I suddenly found that I'd turned into *a young man who'd read a hundred or so books but had never worked an hour in his life,* and I started the long, traditional, and completely useless apprenticeship in the company that so many other young men born into manufacturing families have undertaken before and since, an apprenticeship that is designed in theory to deflate your swelled head and familiarize you with all the various aspects of real factory work. In practice this just wastes precious years during which you're coddled by the real factory workers, and you half-heartedly perform a series of unchallenging tasks that teach you little or nothing: I was assistant foreman in charge of raw materials, assistant technician in charge of mixing and blending fibers, assistant warehouseman, assistant sales director. Assistant everything, once all was said and done.

Once I had completed this Prato version of the ancient Roman *cursus honorum,* or sequence of offices, I was gradually positioned to take over the company. From that point on, my working life began to accelerate, hurtling though a succession of fleeting events, stations on a journey, and the best way I know to describe it to you is to ask you to imagine one of those time-lapse sequences that only the best directors can actually pull off, visually narrating years of a character's life in just a few seconds. Put on a period song (any hit disco song from the period would work just fine, but let's just imagine you choose "Can't Take My Eyes Off You," that heart-swelling song that's featured in *The Deer Hunter,* by Michael Cimino, during the dance scene in the bar, the night before the young men are scheduled to leave the country to go fight the Vietcong), and watch me as I infest the offices of the textile company dressed in jeans and a blazer and a pair of gym shoes, under the fiery gaze of both my father and Alvaro (the son of Alfiero, the grandson of Omero, and the representative of the other branch of the family, with a name that seemed designed specifically to go hand in hand with my father's name, forming the dynamic duo Alvaro & Alvarado, the Prato version of one of those irresistible pairs of stars, like say Roger Moore and Tony Curtis, the *Persuaders!* of the

Italian textile industry), and imagine me dealing with such increasingly high-level corporate issues as:

1. *Checking the shipper's invoices* (I developed a computer program to analyze the invoices on the basis of our shipping rates, which allowed me to identify systematic discrepancies in the invoices, discrepancies that invariably meant we lost money). Here you could feature a shot of me, standing in shirtsleeves as I show something on a computer printout to Alvaro—who is sitting on his desk, wearing a navy-blue jacket and a yellow tie, and nodding thoughtfully.

2. *Estimating stock value* (my brilliant contribution here was to assign specific values to different kinds of partially finished goods, for instance I assigned different values to colored yarns and white threads, the more commonly used raw materials and the less commonly used ones, so that we could develop a more accurate overall valuation of the stock we were warehousing). Here you might feature a shot of me, standing in the raw-materials warehouse that Daniele Vicari later used in the shooting of his documentary *Il mio paese*. I'm wearing a raw-cut navy-blue overcoat and a scarf of some bright color,

I'm looking at a procession of wool bales wrapped
in the jute canvas that the artist Alberto Burri so
loved, and I'm pointing out something to the warehouseman as he pivots around me on his forklift.

3. *Negotiating with the banks* (that was fairly easy, at the
   beginning, because the weaving mill was entirely
   self-financing and the work/challenge was limited
   to the issue of date of valuta on the checks that we
   deposited and the rate of interest on our account;
   it became much more disagreeable later when we
   found ourselves obliged to rely on bank loans,
   something that scandalized my father). I would say
   that here I could be shown sitting in the bare office
   of the young, ambitious, poorly dressed director
   of the local branch office as we shake hands with
   a smile, with sunlight streaming in on us from
   behind, the two of us certainly starting out on what
   would be great careers.

4. *Starting negotiations on the first orders from smaller markets*
   (Portugal, where I went once a year, to the beautiful city of Porto, on the Atlantic coast, where they
   ornament the walls of their buildings with sky-blue
   majolica; or Russia, where, in the aftermath of the
   great crisis that dismembered the empire and which

no one remembers today, they started holding colossal universal expositions in Moscow, trade fairs that I attended without much success; in fact, I spent most of my time talking with my interpreter about the films of Nikita Mikhalkov, because she had taken classes with Mikhalkov during her time at the university and she claimed that for a hundred dollars she could persuade the director to come to the trade fair and visit the Lanificio T.O. Nesi & Figli stand, where he would pose for a photograph with me against the background of our fabrics; another market was the United States, which absolutely refused to show interest in our production). This could constitute the last shot in the passage-of-time editing sequence: now I'm walking down Manhattan's Fifth Avenue, immersed in America's great river of human traffic, but perfectly recognizable by my long curly hair and my Versace houndstooth check jacket; I'm phoning someone, and I'm smiling because everything's going well. A slow fade-out, the song dies down, and there I am sitting at my desk, which is piled high with spreadsheets and samples of raw fabrics, as I tell my father about my latest business trip.

Through a slow, well-managed exit on Alvarado's part from the day-to-day management of the company, I eventu-

ally rose to be the company's co-CEO, alongside Alvaro.
My hair is graying at the temples, I've started wearing a
somewhat scraggly beard. I look happy. I'm just a little over
thirty, I'm married to my beautiful longtime girlfriend, my
first son is about to be born, and my first novel, *Fughe da
fermo*, is about to be published. Once again, I feel sure that
the world is mine, and the only thing missing is a vision
of that phrase written on the side of a blimp sailing slowly
over the Calvana Mountains, at sunset, reading THE WORLD
IS YOURS, like Tony Montana in *Scarface*.

No one could ever have guessed that just a few years later
I'd be selling the company. Of course, it wasn't a decision I
made on my own: Alvaro, who by now was the senior opera-
tive partner, had been involved in every aspect of the negotiations, and he was in agreement; my father Alvarado, who
year by year was spending less and less time on company
business in order to make room for me, was in agreement;
my brothers were in agreement; my family was in agreement; Alvaro's family was in agreement.

We were all in agreement, so we sold the company.

Once negotiations were complete my work was finished,
because, for varied and curious and deeply Italian reasons,
I had never become a partner in the family company of
which I was the CEO, and so I never had to sign the deed
of sale, which instead a baffled and incredulous Alvaro and
Alvarado signed on a hot September afternoon, in the office

of our notary D'Ambrosi, on the Viale della Repubblica in Prato.

I was there, however, and as the notary read aloud the terms of the contract in his delightful Neapolitan lilt and my father and uncle signed, dressed in magnificent linen shirts—navy blue for Alvaro, cream-colored for Alvarado—and the purchasers countersigned, and everyone unfurled their smiles, doing their best to make that strange and never-to-be-repeated encounter as amiable as could be, I was secretly taking pictures of the whole thing, with my cell phone.

Every so often, I look at them, even now.

This History
(Dieter Maschkiwitz)

When you sell a company, you sell its history with it.
And we had a history.

This history.

At the end of the Second World War, as the Germans
were retreating from Prato, they blew up practically all the
textile plants and mills, both large and small. It's hard to
say why without invoking the inborn, callous cruelty of the
German people, a cruelty that ultimately resulted in the
unspeakable acts of that army led by fanatics and zealots
and made up of unfortunates who'd been blinded by the
most demented ideology in human history. Before leaving
the city, they also destroyed the industrial shed that housed
the production facilities of the company of Temistocle and

Omero, bringing roof and walls down on the few pieces of textile equipment that stood inside.

My father, who was nine at the time, witnessed the scene with my grandfather's hand lying heavy on his shoulder. The townspeople of Narnali were rounded up at gunpoint, and then they were given a forced lesson in how German soldiers blow up a factory. Everything that had been painstakingly built up with years of hard work, everything my family owned, vanished in just a few seconds.

Once those Nazi dickheads cleared out, though, Temistocle and Omero set to work immediately to rebuild their company. Slowly, working alongside the rest of Italy, the rest of a country that had likewise been devastated, they scrimped and saved and sacrificed and brought the Lanificio T.O. Nesi & Figli back to life. At first they sold blankets, not fabrics, because it was all they could do to keep up with the Prato companies whose owners had buried their looms to keep them safe from the Germans, as legend would have it, or else had simply been lucky—and thanks to that luck had not been left with their factories in rubble.

The years flew by, as they do whenever an author needs to summarize them in just a few lines. After the death of the founders, the company was run by Alvaro and Alvarado, and our most important market became none other than Germany, as if the heirs to those soldiers felt some sense of guilt for having blown up the factory and were trying to make it up to us as best they could.

They stopped making blankets and specialized in making two kinds of coat material that, due to the long harsh Teutonic winters, never seemed to go out of fashion: velour, that soft fabric with a straight pile that was used to make ladies' winter coats; and loden, a fabric made out of regenerated wool (which is to say, rags) and sold to the Austrians in dozens of shades of green and to other clients in the classic timeless men's colors: charcoal gray, black, and navy blue.

Try to imagine a product that for thirty years never needs to be changed. Imagine a company that only manufactures that product and whose one problem, if it has any problem at all, is that it can't keep up with the demand of a market that is so strong and vast that the threat of competition is not worth worrying about. Imagine being able to set your watch by the punctuality with which invoices are paid ten days from receipt, never a protest, never a deduction for unjustified complaints, never a bankruptcy, with checks pouring in with the morning mail in pastel-hued, square-format envelopes. Zero expense for research and development, trade fairs, advertising, or fashion consultants. Eliminate the very concept of warehouse overstock. Laugh till your belly aches at the idea of having to hire an outside executive to take over the work that you're perfectly capable of doing yourself.

And now try to imagine an entire city based on the textile industry, dotted with dozens and dozens of companies just like ours, all of them growing steadily and all of them intertwined in a system of production that is insanely fragmented but incredibly efficient, made up of hundreds of microcompanies, many of them family-run, each of them working in an intermediate phase of the production and supply chain, each with its own name, its corporate pride, and its profitable balance sheet—perfect little working models of the most exciting dream of capitalism, that exceedingly rare phenomenon that makes capitalism something verging on *morality*, whereby the most skillful and ambitious workers who decide to go into business for themselves had a good chance of succeeding, and thus taking the first step onto a society-wide escalator that never seems to stop climbing upward, creating wealth and distributing that wealth in a way that, while it may not be fair (it's never fair), is at least fine-grained and extensive. But the best thing about it, the truly fantastic thing, is that you didn't have to be a genius to rise to the top, because the system worked so well that even dimwits made money, as long as they were willing to work; even idiots could make money, as long as they dedicated every minute of their days to their work.

In our company, back then, there were no faxes, no computers—there was only the surrealistic telex, something that looked like a giant's typewriter and would suddenly spring mysteriously to life whenever a message arrived: the machine began to vibrate and ring, while the keys began to depress themselves as if being pounded by phantom fingers, cranking out a text that was often made cryptic by abbreviated words, because the cost of telex messages was based on individual characters. The message was almost always an incoming order being placed by the GITA Handelsagentur on Berlin's Geibelstrasse, the military wing of Dieter Maschkiwitz, our agent in Germany, a country that in those days was still split into two parts, the Federal Republic of Germany and the German Democratic Republic. Maschkiwitz, tireless Prussian that he was, traveled the country from north to south and from east to west at the wheel of his BMW 520, taking advantage of Germany's well-known but almost incredible absence of highway speed limits.

He was an odd piece of work, Maschkiwitz was. Surly and intelligent, corpulent and pensive, he had thousands of interests but refused to talk about them until the workday was done. He nurtured a genuine veneration for his elder brother—a mythical figure whom my father had once met, telling me later that he had been struck by the *light of pure intelligence* that burned in the eyes of that solitary man. The brother had never needed to work because he *made money playing the stock market* and lived somewhere in the Southern United States on a floating house of some sort; he had pressed Dieter until Dieter finally bought one for himself, a low-slung, broad-beamed boat that resembled a barge, which he kept moored on Lake Garda, and where I was once a guest, as a child.

On my first business trip to Germany, it was my job to drive my father's Mercedes 500 SE all the way to Munich, where we met with Maschkiwitz and then went together to visit Lodenfrey, in the large plant located right in the middle of the Englischer Garten, or English Garden, the huge park in the center of the city. I witnessed a negotiating session that stretched out for four hours straight, all in German, between Herr Frey, Dieter, and my father, an ordeal that was further complicated by the fact that I had the general impression I hadn't understood a thing. Try as I might to understand their German (not to claim that I spoke the language of Sebald, but after reading all the telexes that poured into our offices, I thought that I'd picked up a smattering of textile-industry vocabulary, at least, and I felt sure that I could recognize technical terminology, when I heard it uttered), it seemed to me that they had spoken for hours about the weather, the German approach to vacationing, which appeared to differ greatly from the holiday habits of the Austrians, the prospects of the Bayern Munich soccer team, and the political maneuvering of Franz Josef Strauss, the Christian Democrat party boss of the Bavaria of those years.

I was pretty sure that they had never once mentioned Pisa fabric, even though we had gone there specifically to sell a hundred thousand linear meters of it to Herr Frey at the moderate price of 16.95 DM per meter. Pisa was a loden fabric weighing 550 grams per linear meter, made up of 72 percent new and regenerated wool and 28 percent polyester, 150 centimeters across between selvages, yarn-dyed, with a KD finish, rendering its pile unalterable and capable of withstanding the assault of Germany's acid rains and terrible morning frosts and snows; the fabric, to be assorted in the classic loden colors, was perfect for making men's overcoats and would last for years and years.

It wasn't until we left the building, long after sunset, and I was driving along the massive Munich beltway, whizzing past the Olympiastadion, that it dawned on me that my attention must have wandered, because we'd gotten the order in the first five minutes—and not at the price we were hoping for, but at ten pfennigs *more*. That's the way Maschkiwitz worked, he wanted to make sure that the company made money, and he was completely unafraid of his customers, and for three hours and fifty minutes, in fact, they had talked about the weather and Bayern Munich and politics because, as my father explained to me, that's the way things work in Germany: sometimes it's just necessary to talk for a while about the weather, about Bayern, and about Strauss.

That same evening, as we were finishing dinner, Maschkiwitz told me that his and Alvarado's chosen profession, a profession that I was now evidently choosing myself, was not one that made a wonderful impression on people. It wasn't a profession that would get you in the news, it was not tremendously fun, it wasn't exciting or illustrious—he said, to be precise, that it's not like being a financier or an airline pilot or a writer—but it was a profitable profession, if practiced properly, and by *properly* he meant conscientiously, seriously, with respect for other people, and it could bring in plenty of money and provide jobs for many people and feed many families, and in his opinion, I'd be good at it, provided I learned German perfectly and always remembered the things he had just told me.

All I could think to do was to nod, ambitiously dressed in the white-and-black houndstooth check Versace jacket that my mother had bought for me and slipped into my suitcase so that I'd at least look like a businessman, awestruck by those solemn words befitting an Indian chief, swelling with pride at the fact that Dieter thought it mattered to speak them to me. I staggered my way back to my hotel room that night, more exhausted than I'd ever been before, after the five hours of driving and the four hours of incomprehensible negotiations and the large stein of *Weissbier* that I'd downed along with the Wienerschnitzel—and yet, not even that night did I fail to read a few grieving pages of *Under the Volcano* by Malcolm Lowry, a book that in those days I carried with me everywhere as if it were the Holy Gospel.

Many years later, Dieter developed a brain tumor, underwent major surgery, and the minute he'd finished convalescing, decided to come to Prato for the last time. He walked into the building with a smile on his face and a hunter's cap on his head to conceal the gift of baldness that chemotherapy had bestowed upon him. Even though I knew that he'd be skinny and older, I stood there, aghast at seeing him *so* skinny and *so* much older, and I couldn't bring myself to welcome him with my usual warmth. I was struck dumb at the sight of him, until he was forced to come toward me, arms outstretched—and it's something for which I've never been able to forgive myself since. He insisted on going out to lunch at Tonio, his favorite restaurant in Prato, in Piazza Mercatale, and he ordered a bowl of *spaghetti con le arselle*—tiny clams—and asked for a bottle of Vernaccia from San Gimignano, and he smiled and talked about business the whole lunch through. When he died not long afterward, the news reached us after the funeral had already taken place, because that's the way he had wanted it. He arranged to be cremated without fuss or ceremony, Dieter did, and his ashes were scattered, I believe, in the North Sea.

Ardently Desired

I never thought for a second that, once we sold the company, I'd be unemployed, or without a job.

The whole time I worked for the weaving mill, I had always desired—ardently desired—to be able to do nothing but write: and I always thought of myself as a writer, even when I was talking with customers and suppliers, with banks and representatives, with our accountant, with our employees, and in fact, my first three novels were largely written on company time, under Alvaro's benevolent eye, as he pretended not to notice what I was doing, in the free time I managed to find during a workday that began at nine and often dragged itself exhausted over the threshold of seven in the evening, because *it just wasn't right for the company to be open without an owner inside.*

Still, all the same, I never felt out of place as a manufacturer: perhaps because I had been programmed in some
sense to enter that profession, or maybe because I happened
to run a company in the last moment of time in which it was
still possible to feel some sense of excitement and enthusiasm *for work*, in that blessed part of Italy where everyone
seemed to move at the frenetic velocity of the little men in
Buster Keaton films.

Because there were times in the life of a young businessman in the late eighties and early to mid-nineties that really
could be exciting, like taking off from Florence airport first
thing in the morning, when it was still dark out, aboard
a Lufthansa Airbus, and flying to Munich or Frankfurt
where Thomas, Dieter Maschkiwitz's titanic son, would be
waiting for me at Arrivals, and we'd sail down the Auto-
bahn in his BMW M5 reaching insane speeds, 170 miles
per hour at times, to make it in time to appointments with
clients where we'd battle ferociously for orders, and then
that same evening we'd go sailing in the opposite direction,
still at 170 miles per hour, toward the airport, where I'd
board the same Lufthansa Airbus and return triumphant
to Florence at eleven that night; or on Friday evenings when
I'd pull up a chair in the warehouse and watch the dizzying
back-and-forth of the workers on the loading dock, scram-
bling to stow hundreds of pieces in the trucks; or when we'd
have fabric assortment meetings and we were all focused on

trying to select the best items for the coming season, and after a while, Sergio Vari, a fantastic fabric designer and a good friend, would get bored and start talking about his time in Goa in 1964, and how close he'd come to never returning to Italy ("I was there, and Led Zeppelin was there"), and rattling on about the fabulous woolen sweaters worn by Fitzgerald characters, or the linen shirts that Hemingway wore in Africa to go elephant hunting, and then I'd start chiming in excitedly that those were exactly the fabrics we should make, the fabrics that writers wore and wrote about, and I'd hurry out to get their books—because I always had an extra copy of the most important works in my office—and Sergio would get worked up and his Bolognese accent would get a little livelier, dropping the second consonant in double-consonant words in his excitement, and the technicians would cluster wide-eyed around the old black-and-white photographs on the backs of the dust jackets, bending closer and peering intently to see just how those fabrics were constructed, and a few weeks later we'd have on the conference table those very fabrics that had been suggested to us by Lowry and Hemingway, and to make a long story short it could be great fun to be a businessman. Especially because in your company everyone does exactly what you tell them to do, whether you're right or wrong.

And so for years, in thrall to an indomitable tendency I have of never wanting to let go of anything, ricocheting endlessly between an ardent passion and a muddled sense of duty, I did my best to avoid making a decision, or perhaps to put off indefinitely my decision until—to use the advice offered to me by Agostino Cesaroni, the Zen *über*-CPA of Pesaro who occasionally came to Prato to fine-tune the balance sheets of my father-in-law and at dinner would tell me how business was going in their industrial district of furniture manufacturers and then force me to play basketball with him until late in the night, one on one, on the terrace outside my house—*until that decision had materialized before my eyes and it was evident to me that no other decision was possible.*

But for eleven years, from 1993 until 2004, nothing materialized before my eyes, and I tried to do both things at the same time, that is, be a manufacturer and a writer, in a fool blend of jobs that aroused the admiration and the envy of my industrialist coworkers—many of whom secretly believed that they had an artist hidden within— and the suspicious bafflement of the writers I was getting to know—many of whom secretly believed deep down that they'd be perfectly capable of running a company.

I kept telling myself that I would go on doing my utmost to have the best of both of the worlds that I was frequenting, using the notions I picked up in one world to work more effectively in the other, all the while ignoring the verdict issued decades earlier by Thomas Pynchon in his least successful novel, the brilliant and unreadable *V,* which is that anyone who has a normal job and tries to make a living while he's writing is convinced that he's getting the best of both worlds, but in fact he's getting only the worst because, since he can never devote himself entirely to one thing, he winds up living a life of expectation, fragmented and interrupted, incomplete and devoid of achievement, a life of fatal unhappiness.

Now that the company has been gone for more than five years—or perhaps I should say, now that it's become someone else's company, and is therefore gone as far as I'm concerned, vanishing from before my eyes and from my awareness—I finally understand that my desire, my yearning for the day when I'd be able to *concentrate on writing*, leaving to others the responsibility for yarns and fabrics and looms, was probably a fundamental part of my way of understanding life: a necessary and childish reaching out toward a multitude of objectives, near and far, important and trivial, which I cannot help but pursue with every ounce of strength I possess, without ever thinking of what I'll do when and if I ever attain them.

And so now, at the most challenging moment in the history of Prato's textile industry, and therefore of Italy's textile industry, and indeed the European textile industry, as I continually receive reports of the serial bankruptcies of German apparel companies that were once as solid as granite bedrock; as each morning's local newspaper brings me the news of the grave difficulties afflicting many of my former fellow industrialists; as the hundreds of craftsmen and artisans who made our sector of the textiles supply chain so great and so special ask nothing more than to be ushered courteously to the exit so that they can decorously fold the microcompanies they founded without losing every penny they've managed to save in decades of hard work; as every year *thousands* of people lose their jobs in my city, which barely has a population of 200,000, if that; as these days total strangers stop me in the street to congratulate me for having sold the company, I cannot help but feel every day a sort of dull heartbreak that seizes me and leads me down a spiraling path into a nameless, full-blown sense of anguish, preventing me from feeling, at last, if not pride, at least relief at having probably spared my family and myself a decline that would have been long, drawn out, and extremely painful, and, considering the way we Nesis are put together, would have erased from our memories all of the good things that we once did and achieved.

I can't manage to get out of my head that *& Figli*—"& Sons"—that seals the end of the name of the woolen mill, that announcement of continuity that was at once an evocation and an invocation, a promise made to me sixty years ago now by a grandfather I never knew. I can't say whether I was a sly fox or a miserable coward, whether I did the right thing or betrayed my birthright, as if the same daring and courage were demanded of a captain of industry as of the captain of a ship, as if it were a moral requirement that he stay with his command until it settles on the bottom of the sea, that he stay with the company that bears his name. I wonder whether it really is possible to love a job, to love a company.

Then, of course, I get over it. I go home and I get over it. I see my wife and my childen, and I get over it. But now I know that it's not enough for me to write novels. It can't be enough for me. I know that I have to try to write *my history and the history of my people*, as Fitzgerald wrote in one of his last desperate letters to his agent, trying to describe *The Love of the Last Tycoon*, the wonderful novel about movies and riches and being in love that he was never able to complete because on December 21, 1940, in the Los Angeles that he did not love, his heart flickered out.

And that's what I'll try to do, before mine flickers out too.

The Fitzgerald Summer

I've always set aside the summer for the kind of reading that most greatly demands one's unbroken attention. There was the summer of *War and Peace*, the summer of *Infinite Jest*, the Dostoyevsky summer, the Pynchon summer and the Salinger summer, the summer of the Bible, the Carver summer. This has been the summer of Francis Scott Fitzgerald's non-novels. All, fearlessly, read in English. No translators, no narrative. Him and me, head to head. His language, his words. His life.

I read the monumental biography, *Some Sort of Epic Grandeur*; the collection of letters, *A Life in Letters*; a collection of short fiction that takes its title from one of his finest short stories, *Babylon Revisited*; the collection of Hollywood short stories, *The Pat Hobby Stories*; and last of all, *The Crack-Up*, a collection of essays and notes and letters—letters both written and received—including many irritated letters from Hemingway and one glacial, perfect note from Edith Wharton, thanking Fitzgerald for having sent her a copy of *The Great Gatsby*, complete with *friendly dedication.*

These readings have done me a world of good. In the shade, on the immaculate beach of a present-day Forte dei Marmi increasingly dazzled by the new, lurid riches of the Russians, I was in the perfect state to work up a childlike enthusiasm and tumble back into my luxuriant habits from before I became a writer, when reading was nothing more than my chief passion: dog-earing pages, reading certain prodigious sections aloud, setting down the book and looking out to sea or up at the sky for minutes at a time, my mind flooded with beauty after reading a perfect passage, occasionally moved to the point of tears.

It was with effort that I kept myself from underlining whole pages at a time, lost as I was in admiration at Fitzgerald's sublime magic, the way he managed to put into words the elusive and nebulous material that so often makes up our finest and most crystalline thoughts, the ones of which we're proudest, the sacred ones, the ones we feel sure are ours and ours alone, private and inexpressible, and inexpressible precisely because they are private: the very essence of our understanding and sensibilities, as well as any author's Holy

Grail, because their understanding lasts only the duration of a spark and then vanishes, incredibly delicate and as fragile as a tropical plant of thought, inevitably leaving behind it a stab of regret that we've lost something crucial. Each time, I sat there gazing into the middle distance, blinking, bewildered, because it's taken me years but I've finally realized that even the greatest inner riches mean little, almost nothing, unless they're expressed, and everything we fail to say or write or live is lost—mere dust.

I'm drinking an aperitif at La Capannina with Angelica, my daughter with eyes the color of the purest cocoa. It's just her and me, the two of us alone, the only customers on the broad veranda, because she loves skating over from the beach and coming here for a before-dinner drink, especially when *La Band* is playing, as they are this evening: a couple of guys in their early thirties, a keyboardist and a guitarist who do covers—remarkably good ones—of old hits by America, James Taylor, Bob Dylan, and Neil Young.

Since the days, twenty years ago as I write this, when I came to spend my most fervent and painful adolescent nights here, La Capannina has became famous as a setting for certain box-office hits starring Christian De Sica and Isabella Ferrari. In fact, the owner of the club proudly proclaims that it is *one of the oldest dance clubs in the world*: it's surprising to hear him make that boast, which anywhere else would be counterproductive at best, even a very good reason to stop going there entirely, but here in Versilia, a tiny, proud, wildly beautiful region in the heart of the Tuscan coastland, it has become just one more of the many instances of yearning for a past that is so distinctive to Forte dei Marmi and its people, an instance of the muddled, cunning desire of an entire city to appear exactly *as it once was*, set in a vague and immensely malleable time that can easily be stretched from the 1920s all the way up to the 1990s, but which always lines up with the happiest years of the rememberer's youth.

Perched on the beachfront, La Capannina looks very much like a big house from the 1930s, the decade in which the old building burned down, only to be rebuilt exactly where it was and as it was, with the wooden shutters and windows and doors all painted green, the pergola over the veranda in front of the bar, the marble floors and the terra cotta stairs, the counter covered with mooring hawsers, and the exquisite hardwood parquet of the dance floor. It's the most powerful and tenacious ghost in this small town that lives off ghosts, selling you another scrap of your own memories every day, and charging top dollar each time.

It hasn't been a very good day.

There's a billboard announcing a Back-to-the-Eighties Night with Jerry Calà, who looms large in the photograph, with a microphone in one hand and a stolid gaze, and I wonder to myself how or when Jerry Calà, of all people, ever became the proprietor of the eighties in Forte dei Marmi, considering the fact that I never saw him there back then— that same Jerry Calà who has battened off the incredible, unmistakable collapse of intelligent thought in the realm of popular music (no, make that pop, I'd prefer to describe it as *pop* music) over the past twenty years, the same Jerry Calà who every night fills the house with kids excitedly humming the hit songs of Lucio Battisti and Edoardo Vianello, Gino Paoli and the Ricchi e Poveri, Gianni Morandi and the Righeira, all churned together into a chowder that he could never have performed in the eighties without being booed off the stage, even though today, that same stew is the basis of his popularity; the Jerry Calà who, when he sings "Io vagabondo" by the Nomadi, every so often changes the verse that goes "but high up above me, I still have God," into "but high up above me, I still have Silvio"; that Jerry Calà, the one from the Gatti di Vicolo Miracoli.

It *really* hasn't been a very good day.

During my enervating daily walk down the beach, as I go slaloming among and around the bathers shouting and smoking and splashing in the salt water and laughing about nothing at all, the children crying because they've got sand in their eyes and the mothers hurrying to comfort them and the old men who seem possessed of wisdom only because they sit silently looking out to sea, I couldn't keep myself from wondering what all these people were going to do when their jobs vanished into thin air, as they were soon bound to do.

And what about me? What am I going to do?

I watch as Angelica whirls on her roller skates from the buffet to our table, conveying plates loaded high with canapés without ever dropping one. She brakes to a halt and sits down in a single fluid movement, my doll baby. She must have noticed I was lost in thought, maybe she thinks I'm worried, and she touches my arm and asks me whether the song that has just started is by Neil Young, who has surprisingly become her brother Ettore's favorite singer, so that our communal iPod is now filled with old Neil Young songs ("Harvest," "Old Man," "Heart of Gold," "A Man Needs a Maid," and, first and foremost, "After the Gold Rush"). I tell her no, "A Horse with No Name" is by America.

We place our orders. I ask for a martini and she gets a peach smoothie, and Angelica asks me, "Listen, Dad, why aren't we looking at the sunset right now? I mean, why is La Capannina turned around to face the mountains instead of toward the sea?"

I tell her that I have no idea, but that she has a point: we're overlooking the Apuan Alps, the two of us, and the marble cliffs are tinged pink from what must be a spectacular sunset, a sunset we can't see because it's on display behind us, on the far side of the mass of La Capannina.

Maybe it's because, back when they built the place, it was common belief that at day's end, fine ladies and gentlemen had all had their fill of the glittering Tyrrhenian Sea and the bright sunshine and the gentle breezes and would therefore choose to relax in the shade, resting their eyes on the fleeting apparitions of young women riding bicycles past the club, pedaling quickly with downcast eyes in a rustle of skirts; or on the daring streamlining of the deluxe custom cars parked ostentatiously outside the club; or even on the cooling view of those very same Apuan Alps, with their pink marble, the ones my doll baby and I are gazing upon right now. On the spectacle of summer's riches and youth, in other words. A rather Fitzgeraldian conceit, if I say so myself.

Ah, Fitzgerald!

As a young man, Scott (because no one but his mother ever called him *Francis*) wrote about Zelda: "I was in love with a whirlwind and I must spin a net big enough to catch it out of my head, a head full of trickling nickels and sliding dimes, the incessant music box of the poor . . ." And Zelda seemed to be replying to him, many years later, in a letter from the Swiss psychiatric clinic where she had wound up: "Scott, I love you more than anything on earth and if you were offended I am miserable . . . please love me—life is very confusing—but I love you."

The waiter brings my martini and, before taking my first sip, which is invariably the best due to certain incontrovertible laws of physics, I take a couple of seconds to inhale the wonderful scent of cologne that emanates from the glass of a properly concocted martini—made, that is, with Tanqueray gin and an infinitesimal dash of vermouth. This is the ideal weapon if you want to hurt yourself fast, and I gulp it down, on an empty stomach, practically all at once. It unfailingly works.

The band starts a cover of "The Needle and the Damage Done," and Angelica glances in my direction to inquire whether this one is by Neil Young and I answer yes, this one yes, and as she starts singing along softly under her breath, I summon my ghosts to take their places at all the empty tables at La Capannina. They arrive in no time at all and sit down around me and Angelica, ignoring us as if we were the phantoms, instead of them. Dressed in Irish linens and gleaming cottons, handsome and fragile, jejune and remote, cunning and ravenous, naive and ignorant, they are the cream of the crop of that exceptionally fortunate generation of Italians without any special training, enthusiastic and insurrectionist, that was lucky enough to venture onto the world stage just at the dawning of an era of unbridled economic expansion destined to last for decades, ultimately culminating in the creation of a market of hundreds of millions of *Western* consumers—women and men with a lust for life, overjoyed to have survived a world war and eager to rebuild a world from the rubble and immediately start living again and earning money and spending it, because this was the beginning of a period of progress and man was walking on the moon, and the future was certain to be a thousand times better and more prosperous than the present.

And there they are, my fathers and my brothers. My mothers and my sisters. I've always lived with them, I've always written about them. There they are, drinking their martinis and their negronis and their camparis and their gin-and-tonics, calm and complacent, tipsy and contented, already rendered lazy by their youthful money, miserably happy with all that they possess, their houses at Forte dei Marmi and their Ferraris, their boats and their elegant clothing, their factories and their spectacular lovers, with everything that must have seemed so much to them while in fact it was very little, the very least that could be obtained by spending all that money.

I feel like leveling with them, telling them that instead of playing at being industrialists and building one factory after another, piling up transitory fortunes, they might at the very least have tried taking a look around them at the extraordinary period of flourishing arts and letters, all blossoming practically within reach, the seething twentieth century of the arts, because if they had, it might *somehow have become possible* to turn this process of savage flourishing into an industrial idea, then actual products, and then wealth, perhaps by linking up with the universally held certainty that Italy is the cradle of worldwide creativity, that splendid old chestnut that still seems to work everywhere around the world and which has deep roots extending back in time to the earliest era, to that never-to-be-repeated moment when life and art blended so intimately—the Florentine Renaissance, when Lorenzo de' Medici engendered and perpetuated the idea that the Italians possess a special kind of brilliant artistic spirit that makes them unlike any other people in terms of their ability to draw inspiration from art and bring it down to earth in the form of a sublime and unrivaled artisanry.

I couldn't say, perhaps that's pure bullshit.

I order another martini and look over at my little girl. We're both exhausted, she and I. The air has freshened, it's almost September. "The Needle and the Damage Done" comes to an end, and Angelica and I both applaud the performance. The second martini shows up in a flash, it seems. This one is even better than the first, and I say so to the kind and courteous waiter, who could serve as a stand-in for the great soccer coach Arrigo Sacchi, and for an instant—and it truly is just a fleeting instant—as my baby doll looks out over the Apuan Alps and the icy chill of my glass anesthetizes my fingertips and the gin plummets dizzyingly down my throat, I experience happiness: I'm profoundly and incomprehensibly happy, for no good reason, and I have to close my eyes, and all the ghosts vanish, and when I open them again there's no one around me but Angelica.

She asks me the name of the song they've just started playing. She loves this song; her brother has played it for her before, and I tell her it's "Knockin' on Heaven's Door" by Bob Dylan, and even though the music is loud and this isn't the time for it and it's completely out of left field and we have to get going, I wish I could tell her how wonderful it would be if right now it were possible for *culture* to rescue Italy. What a dream that would be. If only novels and movies and paintings and poetry and opera and songs and even fashion—yes, even fashion—could ride to the rescue, preserving jobs and saving us all from a long, steady slide into, first, depression and ultimately poverty. I'd even be willing to go ask those clowns, the fashion designers, to lend a hand: the same ones who demanded discounts on the fabrics we sold them only to mark up their overcoats so that retail was ten times cost of production; the designers who gabbled on endlessly about the Made in Italy label, only to then have the actual garments produced in China, but if anyone pointed that out, they'd fly into a rage and object, yes, but the *concept* still came from Italy; the designers who had always managed to exploit that idea of culture that they'd never personally espoused; the designers who held their runway presentations on the Spanish Steps so that the beauty of the ages might dust their dresses and suits and shoes and bags and eyeglasses, which they then sold off to suckers around the world, unfortunates who, blinded by the magnificence of the frosting, fooled themselves into believing that they really could buy it—all that beauty.

Because all of us need beauty—we need it desperately. But I can't bring myself to use the word *desperately*. Not in front of my daughter, not even after my second martini. So I take her hand and, with the tune of Dylan's song in the background, ask whether she wouldn't like to inhabit a world where everyone could live on culture alone, a wonderful world where you could pay the butcher with a short story, the barkeep with a poem, or even build a house for yourself with a novel—and she laughs and says what a beautiful fairy tale that would be, indeed, and tells me I ought to put it all in a book, this whole thing about a world that runs on culture.

I drain the last drops of my second martini, the drops that cling stubbornly to the sides of the glass, and I wonder whether when it's all said and done what I love most is the martini itself or whether I'm just another victim of its potent mythology, of having read that martinis are what Dick Diver and his wife Nicole drank in *Tender Is the Night*. Then there is the formidable story about Hemingway out having drinks with Gene Tunney, the world heavyweight champion of the twenties who twice defeated Jack Dempsey, and how after his second martini he challenges Tunney to punch him in the stomach. When Tunney refuses, Hemingway persists and starts raising his voice, becoming so quarrelsome that in the end Tunney gives in, if you really insist, I'll throw the punch. And so Hemingway gets to his feet, clenches his gut, shouts out that he's ready, and Tunney punches him in the belly and Hemingway falls to the ground and lies there motionless, eyes closed, for a good ten minutes, as if he's dead. But then when he finally gets back on his feet, he's docile and good tempered, ready to be a good boy, and there's no more shouting.

And then there's the memorable line attributed to Winston Churchill who said that the way to make a perfect martini is to look intensely for a few seconds at a bottle of dry vermouth, and then pour iced gin over an olive in a diamond-cut crystal martini glass.

I close my eyes, I inhale and exhale, and when the song comes to an end, we applaud again. It's time to get up and pay, then I'll have to focus, get on my bike, and escort my roller-skating doll baby home. I pray that I'll be able to walk with dignity, without staggering. Above all things, I hate to stagger.

At the end of his life, Fitzgerald wrote in desperation to his agent, begging for a loan: "Everything I have ever done or written is me."

He wrote his beloved daughter Scottie urging her to continue her studies at Princeton with the greatest possible dedication, and never, ever, ever to take so much as a drink, otherwise he would go on such a massive bender that reports of his colossal drunk would reach her all the way from California.

And fifteen days before his death, Scott Fitzgerald, in his last letter to Zelda, wrote that "everything is my novel."

Shaking the Gates

A few years ago—I was still working for the company, so it must have been 2003 or 2004—I wrote a letter to Francesco Giavazzi, a leading economist and editorialist for the *Corriere della Sera*, perhaps the most die-hard Italian advocate of the infinite bounty of globalization, the man who more than anyone else, in his austere articles that were as relentlessly punctual as death itself, scoffed at the inability of most Italian industrialists to adapt to the new rules of the marketplace, rules imposed by what he considered to be the great and benevolent panacea of a world opening up to free trade.

Up to this point, all clear. He was merely the most insistent of the many economists on all sides who were pouring out their decrees and verdicts on the gloomy prospects of Italian manufacturing, and even though it physically hurt me to read each piece, because he never seemed to tire of singing the praises of each and every factor that to my mind was working day by day to break the back of the small businessman, by the time I finished one of his editorials I was invariably torn by guilt and doubts. Guilt because I wasn't doing—because I *couldn't* do—what he, the professor of economics, was urging businessmen like me to do. Doubts because it is infinitely difficult to maintain your own personal opinion about any given topic when *the whole world* seems to have a different and diametrically opposed view of things, and when they hammer at you all day and every day from all directions, until even the most independent-minded person imaginable starts to give in. And I—who am certainly *not* the most independent-minded person on earth, and in fact, if anything I've always boasted that I'm willing to change my mind on a dime if someone can show me where and how I'm mistaken—was beginning to wonder more and more frequently, as I lay my copy of the *Corriere della Sera* down on the passenger seat of my car and went upstairs to the office, whether Giavazzi might not be right, and I might not be wrong after all.

After all, I told myself, he's a professor of economics, and what am I? Perhaps the last and the youngest of Italy's conservatives, and therefore one of the worst: a blind man, incapable of seeing and grasping and exploiting what was promising to be a momentous and positive change in the world economy; yet another of the countless spoiled brats unwilling to be dragged out of the cashmere cocoons in which they had luxuriated until now, still determined to defy history and defend an anachronistic and protectionistic position toward an age-old system of textile production that was doomed to be swept away by modern globalization; some kind of ridiculous latter-day Luddite, indeed, the last living descendant of old Ned Ludd, whose name has come to symbolize all the irrational and glorious revolts that have ever been destined to fail, while captivating the imaginations of the young and the callow—Ned Ludd, the legendary berserker who ravaged mechanical looms, a man who may never have even existed, for that matter, possibly nothing more than a nom de guerre used by wrecking crews of starving weavers who had watched aghast as their ancient, precious handwork was torn from their grip, and so they reacted by leading the charge against the new mechanized factories of England in the first half of the nineteenth century, the reckless hotheads who were slaughtered wholesale by the king's armies, a king who had grown tired of their onslaughts and mayhem, and who, after executing the leaders of the revolt, ordered the rest to be jailed and then deported to Australia; the rebels who set fire to the new mechanical looms in the name of Ned Ludd or, with far more striking imagery, *King Ludd*, as Byron called him in a famous ode, referenced in an essay by, of all writers—well, well, here he is again—Thomas Pynchon.

My dislike for Giavazzi grew exponentially when, in his many articles that invariably appeared on the front page of the *Corriere della Sera*, he would find an Italian company that was prospering in spite of the hard times and hold it up as a triumphal success story and an example to be emulated by all the rest of us, who were just so many fatheads clearly sitting around twiddling our thumbs as we settled into the morass of decline, and the straw that broke the camel's back came when he started singing the praises of Cotonificio Albini, a major textile firm in Northern Italy that was doing so well, even in the midst of the stark downturn for Italy and all of Europe, that it was able to reinvest a substantial sum in new looms to install in its Italian plants, alongside the vast number it already possessed.

Evidently, we businessmen of Prato were nothing more than a gang of idiots. I saw red and so, swept away by a wave of fury and envy, I wrote him a letter. There was an e-mail address at the bottom of his editorial, but I never sent it in. I figured he wouldn't bother to read it, because e-mails count and will always count less than letters, and no one even bothers to read letters anymore. I decided to allow the simple act of writing the letter to sop up my anger and quench my urge to respond, to raise my voice on behalf of all the businesspeople in the textiles sector who, after being pummeled by a treacherous market, were being asked to see insult piled atop injury as they were pilloried every other day in the pages of the *Corriere della Sera* by Professor Giavazzi.

The idea—deeply naive, I acknowledge—was to do my best to employ what small literary reputation I could bring to bear to win a public hearing on a platform equivalent to that enjoyed by the professor. To strike a blow, in some sense. To bring other voices to a one-sided debate. To stand up on behalf of those who weren't actually all that thrilled about being shoved willy-nilly onto the playing fields of world trade, and not out of any sort of ideological persuasion but for purely pragmatic considerations, because of the sheer terror that not only was this not to the advantage of most of the Italian economy but indeed might very well prove fatal, because I felt that not only was I speaking up for myself and my small company and my personal fears, but also for the thousands of small businesses with their tens of thousands of employees scattered across the country, and their very large fears.

I wanted to try to achieve the literary equivalent of what the Prato soccer hooligans did one long-ago winter Sunday evening, after a match in which a beardless stripling of a referee had looted our team of its rightful score with a series of incredible calls, when thirty or so ultras, led by the legendary Tacabanda, headed off to the apartment building where Sergio Gonella, a great and revered soccer referee of the past who had since become the director of a bank as well as the head of all Italian referees, lived in a rented apartment. They seized the heavy metal gates and began shaking them with the shouts and all the force of a medieval siege.

I lived across the street from where Gonella lived, and when I heard the clangor of that wrought iron gate on the verge of being ripped off its hinges by a phalanx of furious men I was seized by an unreasoning age-old terror, as if something verging on a medieval memory had taken possession of me and driven me to hide in a broom closet somewhere.

I wanted to shake the *Corriere della Sera*'s and Giavazzi's gates. I wanted to give them an idea, if only for a few minutes, of what it feels like to live under siege for years at a time, which is what had happened to me and to nearly all the entrepreneurs in Italy and all their employees, but as I was writing that letter I was seized by a sense of complete futility, and I leveled with myself that there was absolutely no chance that any letter I might write would be published by the *Corriere della Sera*, which in contrast in those days was devoting substantial space to certain deep ideological debates on the deplorable evil of part-time work, just one of the symptoms, and not even the most troubling one, of the complete opening up of trade—the most harmful symptom, obviously, being the complete *elimination* of jobs represented by the unbroken chain of firings to which we stand unwilling and astonished witnesses today. What I had originally conceived as a mighty and indignant hammer blow was snipped and trimmed down until it became little more than a pinprick, but one that pleased me at the time and continues to please me now. I never sent it, but I never deleted it either. It just sat there, buried in the bowels of my computer, hidden but not forgotten, and to reread it today it strikes me as amusing, and still needful. In particular, the detail I like above all is the earnest, dignified signature: *Edoardo Nesi, businessman in Prato,* even though by then I practically no longer was one and perhaps, in a certain sense, I never really had been.

Here it is.

Dear Giavazzi,

Last night I had a dream. I was you, Francesco Giavazzi, and I was free to mock from my pulpit on the front page of the Corriere della Sera *those idiot Italian industrialists who are being torn limb from limb by the Chinese, in the certainty that no one would raise a finger to defend them. It was a wonderful feeling, I was proud to know that I'd figured everything out, and how I lit into them, those knuckleheads: "What the fuck are you waiting for, just shut your businesses down now, dunderheads all of you! Go on: fire all those old blue-collar imbeciles and hire young mathematicians! We need to investigate the new modal interactions between human beings and high technology!"*

Then I woke up screaming: "The Cotonificio Albini! Daddy, the Cotonificio Albini! We need to make a rush order for new looms!" and my wife got scared and it took hours to calm her down.

Edoardo Nesi,
businessman in Prato

The Most Beautiful Fabrics
on Earth

Those were the days when I was still angry, the days just before and after the turn of the new millennium. The company's revenue was dropping year after year, month after month, and I'd come home seething with rage at the bidding wars that by now our clients were forcing us to engage in to land the biggest orders, without any consideration for the quality of the fabrics, the reliability of the service, the on-time deliveries, the company name, the company's history. It was as if our clients had all gone deaf. Even the Germans.

All that mattered anymore was the price, and we were always sure to lose on the price, because there was bound to be someone somewhere whose desperation was greater than ours—someone in Prato, let me be clear, not someone in

Wenzhou—and who had swallowed hook, line, and sinker the enthusiastic, pernicious theories according to which it's always and only the free market that makes the proper decision on the price of any given goods, and so, because *we can't afford to lose that order*, they'd go on lowering the price of their fabrics, until profit had narrowed to the point of vanishing entirely. At that point, we would simply step away from the bidding, losers, perhaps, but still firmly convinced of the truth of that sacrosanct ancient principle according to which, if you're not making a profit, you're surely making a loss.

But the bidding war just went on without us, wicked and stupid as ever, and so the time came when the desperate businessman had to brush back his bangs and climb into his Mercedes ML or his Audi (they always seem to buy those damned, muscular German cars) and go off to throttle the small businessmen who were even more desperate than him, the ones who would actually have to spin and weave, so that he could offer his clients an even lower price, in a perverse spiral that revealed the dirty face of the idea of free-market capitalism and seemed devoted to an insane attempt to guarantee—in Prato—the same cost savings that could be obtained by moving production elsewhere—as if Prato, with its centuries of manufacturing fabrics, might somehow be turned overnight into a piece of Transylvania—and so the artisans found themselves forced to work at prices from the 1980s, in a demented race to the bottom in terms of prices—the race to *Romanian* prices—anything, just to snag the order, victims of a madness that seemed to be infecting the entire city, and sidelining us ineluctably, we, the Lanificio T.O. Nesi & Figli S.p.A., marginalizing us, making us antiquated.

And so, self-propelled and self-fulfilling, the certainty spread unstoppably that, with no one making profits, *the textile industry no longer had a future.* Businessmen wound up abdicating their creative role—because, believe me, if there is a creative and romantic line of work, it's unquestionably that of the entrepreneur—and turned into a herd of terrified pants-wetters, prisoners of an accountant's mindset, a mentality that they'd always dismissed scornfully in the past. They wound up setting aside the freedom of thought that had once helped them to build their savage, pagan industries out of thin air, forgetting the miraculous intuition that once allowed them to see a business opportunity where no one else could glimpse it, the feral clairvoyance that pricked them until they lay awake all night, the certainty that the future was something they could—they had to—build with their own hands, to their own measure, lest their future be tailored for them by others.

Sucker-punched by a decline as sudden and vicious as the bite of an asp, obsessed by the nightmare that their companies, which had always reliably spewed out money in the past, had become in just a few years so many cursed money-gobbling devices, in their terrible waking dreams the businessmen were as tormented by the total costs of their employees as Hamlet was by ghosts. Because if the salaries they were paying every month, along with all the damned benefits costs, had become intolerable burdens, the true nightmare was the expense of *trattamento di fine rapporto;** and so they began telling themselves that perhaps they didn't need all the people who really just got in the way at the start of each day. So they developed the habit of firing employees, in many cases at random, as long as they could cut costs, and among those costs the worst bugaboo was the specter of general outlays: the structural costs, fixed and immutable and eternal, that rise every day and have to be paid no matter what, for instance passive interests, the rent on their industrial sheds, electric bills and heating bills, and all the taxes, including that truly punitive tax dreamed up by the first Prodi administration under the auspices of the then-minister of finance, the ineffable Vincenzo Visco, a tax that bears the name of IRAP but which in Prato has been dubbed IRAQ for the similar wave of devastation it has unleashed. This infernal contrivance obliges you to pay not

---

* An Italian legal institution in which a company retains a certain percentage of an employee's salary each month and uses this money for cash flow. Upon the employee's retirement, resignation, or dismissal, the retained money is returned to the employee, with interest.

on the basis of the profits you may have made, but instead on the basis of the revenue you take in and the number of employees that you have and the interest that you pay to the banks and the losses on credits that you're forced to absorb; an old tax created with the justifiable intent of targeting the earnings of tax evaders but which is now simply massacring struggling companies everywhere, a tax that's seen as the supreme form of injustice because businesses are forced to pay taxes even when they really are making only losses.

And so the businessmen, cursing themselves and their customers and their employees and the downturn and globalization and all the Giavazzis in the world who, instead of helping them, just made fools of them and mocked them with their advice to fire their factory workers and hire young mathematicians, now simply turned up their noses at the idea of spending time in the very same factory where just a few years ago they had even gone on Saturdays and Sundays, and not to do anything in particular, but just to spend a tranquil afternoon surrounded by their possessions and reassured by their role. Now instead they frantically boarded and deboarded planes in a search for orders from every corner of the planet, and once they had reached the far side of the globe from Prato and discovered that there was no way to get any further from their destiny and their company, then they picked up the phone and called *me*, drunk and discombobulated from jet lag. They would tell me about nights when they couldn't sleep because of the heat or the cold or the loneliness, or even just because of the tidal waves of thoughts that overwhelmed them, and they'd tell me that I did the right thing by selling the company, and that they'd taken my book with them on their travels and they were reading this *fantastic* part about Ivo Barrocciai, which is why they'd called me, to tell me how much they'd enjoyed it and then, every time, every last one of them would stop because, drunk though they were, they'd realized that they'd said too much, and with a few hasty salutations and best wishes they'd hang up, sorry they'd called me in the first place.

They would rush to plunge headlong into every damned bidding war that came along without any regard for the final price they accepted for the job, uncaring that by this point they were trussed up and ready to hand themselves over to the giant corporations of the world garment industry. These titanic foreign multinationals, so lionized by business reporters and columnists, sell their heartless, unimaginative rags and *shmattes* everywhere around the world and are the true beneficiaries of globalization; they sell to the masters of our global, fear-quaking world, to buyers who rightly believe that a product's ideal price is determined by the marketplace and the marketplace alone, because in the end they are the marketplace. The multinationals promise us the illusion of fashion at rock-bottom prices, Giorgio Armani at Walmart costs; they entrust their corporate image to full-page ads in newspapers and magazines populated with smiling multi-ethnic youngsters who are bubbling over with happiness and youth and color. The global corporations seem to honor our small businesses with their huge orders but instead are throttling them to death on the unit price; they hunker down in their glittering new general headquarters that have been created for them by their most devotedly loyal slave boys, the renowned architects of the world: jejune, sterile monuments made of steel and cement and glass in such a way that they mirror the sky and the clouds, places where only executives and clerical staff work because the actual production of garments now takes place in a distant corner of the world, in factories that are as different as different can be—trust me, I've seen them—and made by people who are entirely different too, who not only never make it into the advertising pages, but don't even have the money to buy themselves a copy of the magazines that carry the advertisements placed by their generous employers. These giants of apparel, in other words, are listed on every stock exchange on earth, are managed by firm hands (and by *cruel* hands, how tempted I am to write that they have *cruel* hands), and earn *hundreds of millions of euros* every year, while their Italian suppliers, that is, the companies that produce *the most beautiful fabrics on earth*, are forced to lay off employees and swear to falsehoods so they can file an end-of-year balance sheet that shows them breaking even, otherwise the banks will lunge at their throats like so many jackals.

And there is no one, no one, no one at all willing to utter a single word to point out how wrong and stupid and false it is that fabric—by far the most important component of any article of clothing, apparel's very substance and essence, its material form and its dominant image, the first thing a person sees and touches, the principal reason why you decide whether or not to buy—should be so deeply devalued that it constitutes only a minimum part of the cost of any given article of clothing, while the decidedly preponderant portion of that cost is represented by the profits enjoyed by the manufacturer with cruel hands and the costs of the advertisement with the smiling young people!

And that's how we enter the terminal phase of the history of the small Italian textile business, when a healthy metabolic state of competition, a fair battle for profits, is replaced by a furious battle to wrest away nothing more than a lukewarm, increasingly eked-out survival; when entrepreneurs feel consoled by the mere fact that they can get up every morning and go in and continue to work in their factories, that they can continue to call themselves and have others call them industrialists when in fact they do nothing but ape their own recent pasts, without noticing that they're starting to resemble Romero's zombies, which long after their deaths keep going to the supermarket because that's all they remember doing when they were alive.

These lines too are a few years old. Maybe you can tell. As I told you, I was always, always angry. Every day. One time I was ejected from the soccer field where I was serving as a linesman in a match my seven-year-old, Ettore, was playing in. It was Prato versus Empoli, and I'd like to take this opportunity to apologize to all the people who saw me as the referee was waving a red card in my face for something extremely (and I mean extremely) inappropriate that I'd shouted at the top of my lungs about a goal scored by Empoli after time had expired.

The rope of my tolerance and my rage slid through my fingers until I reached the end of that rope, and I started keeping a very heavy steel bar that I'd found in the weaving mill in my car, under the front seat, and as a result my father Alvarado, for the first time in his life, was regarded with suspicion and fear when he took the car in for a tune-up and the mechanic found the bar and showed it to him without mustering the courage to ask him what it was for.

It's not like I had any idea what I would do with it, the steel bar, nor did I have enemies who were looking for me, much less anyone I was looking for myself. I just kept it there, under the seat, and every so often I'd reach down and touch it. It was always chilly to the touch, even in the summer.

And every time I read Giavazzi in the *Corriere della Sera*, I kept thinking of the Twin Towers and the bloodcurdling thing that happened, they say, after the first plane hit. I don't even know if it's true. I hope it isn't.

Apparently, through some kind of public address system, a voice informed everyone inside the building, which was already in flames, that the situation was under control. That they shouldn't give in to panic. That they should stay calm, stay put, and wait for help.

Now, just try to imagine the situation. Try to put yourself in their shoes. You know that an airliner has just plowed into the tower you're in, and you also know that a fire is raging, a few stories over your head. Your immediate instinct is to run down the stairs, as fast as a frightened deer. But just as you're about to take to the stairs, a voice comes over the public address system, telling you that the best thing to do is nothing, just wait for help to come.

Stay where you are, you're told over and over again.

So you freeze, and you try to think things through.

You tell yourself, of course, it's true, you should never give in to panic.

You tell yourself that situations like these have been planned for, and you feel comforted by the fact that, just minutes after impact, there's *already* someone speaking to you over the public address system. That must mean that someone is *already* taking care of the situation.

You tell yourself that the fire trucks must *already* be on their way, that all the firemen in New York are *already* hurrying to the scene and they'll quickly put out the fire.

It's a chain of *already*s that you've knotted one to the next in order to avoid the idea of having to make the decision for yourself, to have to fend for yourself unaided. You tell yourself that it must be true, that you need to keep calm, and it might even be interesting to see how they put out a fire on the eightieth floor.

Because, of course, you're on the eightieth floor. Even if you decided to walk downstairs, it would be an endless succession of steps. It would take you forever, and you know perfectly well that when a building's on fire, you can't use the elevators.

You tell yourself that if everyone started racing down the stairs, all they'd do is prevent help from reaching your floor. Because that's how the firemen would get up here, of course. By the stairs.

Your cell phone no longer works.

No one can help you, you'll have to make your own decision.

And *incredibly*, even though you know that the building is in flames over your head, even though you're beginning to hear all around you obscene screeching noises that seem to come out of the walls, noises unlike anything you've ever heard in your life, even though there's a part of you that keeps asking what the hell you're doing in a building that's on fire, in the end you decide to show *respect for authority*, for the voice of a total stranger that reaches you over the public address system telling you not to give in to panic and to stay where you are.

And you die.

Does this have anything to do with small-scale Italian manufacturing, with my city, with my people?

I don't know. Maybe it does.

Three Literary Souvenirs

I.

"My life is a crystal tear-drop," Joan Baez once said. I learned of this quote from Didion, the wonderful Joan Didion, six of whose finest books I read during this hard winter, one after another, in English, in a state of admiration and disbelief: *The White Album, Slouching Towards Bethlehem, The Year of Magical Thinking, A Book of Common Prayer, Democracy,* and *Play It As It Lays*; Joan Didion, to whom I could hardly keep from writing an enthusiastic e-mail, the e-mail of a genuine fan, in which I told her that in her hands literature became something precious and alive, surgically precise and at the same time set like a jewel in *our heart of hearts*, something very very similar to magic; the same Joan Didion to whom I wrote: *"All your books are gems full of other gems, but I must say that the pages in which you tell the story of Inez flying Jack's body over the Pacific to Schofield, with that precious line about the Italian soldiers incredibly buried there, will always stay in my heart as one of the most elegant and moving descriptions of love lost I have ever read."*

Joan Didion answered my e-mail immediately, the same day she received it. She wrote words of appreciation—*Thank you so very very much*—and told me that I had brightened a dark and chilly New York City Monday. I imagined her smiling briefly as she read my e-mail in the clean white New York apartment that I've seen in so many photographs, wrapped in a milk-white cashmere shawl, she who has suffered so much in her life, because just possibly my sincere and enthusiastic praise for a book she had written twenty-five years earlier might have brought back to her a happier moment.

I owed her my gratitude, because it was thanks to her, the author who, in *Democracy*, has a spectacular war profiteer buried under a jacaranda tree at Schofield Barracks in Hawaii, adding that past that tree are the graves of the Italian soldiers, which piqued my curiosity, so I did an Internet search and found the incredible story of five thousand Italians who were taken prisoner by British troops in North Africa, during the Second World War, only to be handed over for some reason to the Americans, who then went to the trouble of loading them onto transport planes and bringing them first to a detention center in Seattle and from there to Schofield Barracks in Hawaii, on the far side of the world. Before long they realized their Italian prisoners were harmless and gave them free rein of the base, to work as gardeners and cooks, and one of them, Alfredo Giusti from Pietrasanta, even took up stone carving, and sculpted two marble statues—the first one dedicated to his girlfriend, the second to a Hawaiian beauty—and two fountains—one adorned with the winged lion of Venice and the other crowned by pineapples: an artist who first sculpted the things he missed and later the things he saw.

I thought for a long time about those Italian soldiers, infinitely far from home, prisoners in the most beautiful place on earth, between the Bismarck palms and the Pacific Ocean, in a true and Polynesian version of that little Italian movie that won an Oscar, *Mediterraneo*, and I had even considered the idea of making a stab at completing the circle and tearing open the golden wrapping that concealed the gift that Joan Didion had given me, because someone from Versilia always eventually returns home, and Pietrasanta is close to Prato and that's where my brother Lorenzo lives. So I set out to track down Giusti so I could ask him about being a prisoner in paradise and then tell you what he said in this book, which I would then have translated and sent to Joan Didion in New York, but it turns out that our artist-soldier died at the turn of the 1990s, sadly, taking with him his memories and his wonderful story of a Pietrasantese prisoner in paradise.

2.

Hanging framed on the wall behind me is a sheet of notebook graph paper on which David Foster Wallace answered one of my questions about *Infinite Jest* in his vivid and punctilious style.

I had asked Martina Testa (the editorial director of the publishing house minimum fax) to ask him whether or not Don Gately dies at the end of the novel, and he wrote me:

> *To Edoardo.*
> *I had a version of an early draft where D.G. died, but the version had terrible problems . . . so I think it's more true that he doesn't die (there are 3 clues in the final version that he does not).*

He ended the note with a *Ciao* followed by an exclamation mark, and his signature, and then he entrusted the note to our very dear mutual friend, and every time that I look at that sheet of paper, I take comfort from that exclamation mark, an uncommon thing for him, and I imagine him in the throes of one of his very rare moments of serenity, DFW, on Capri, in the summer, in the presence of a sun and a sea more beautiful than anything he'd ever seen before, surrounded by eager admirers, and that's the way I

always try to remember him, the most remarkable writer
I've ever read and translated, the suicide who taught me to
live.

3.

In my computer I still have four pictures that depict me
with Richard Ford. They were taken in 2007, in the *Corriere della Sera*'s Sala Buzzati, during the Milanesiana, immediately after a public conference where we were invited to
speak along with Piergiorgio Odifreddi, the mathematician,
and Thomas Crombie Schelling, 2005 Nobel laureate in
economics.

I never prepare for conferences or speeches, so I never
know what I'm going to say until it's my turn to speak.
Those are valuable moments. I enjoy feeling simultaneously
the awareness that my head is completely empty, the thrill
of fear that I'll open my mouth and nothing will come out,
and the almost total certainty that that won't happen. My
heartbeat races when I'm given the floor and I smile, I greet
the audience, and I slide into those brief, exquisite seconds
of mental void when I still don't know what I'm going to say,
a scant arc of silence inside which I sometimes think I'd be
happy to live, perfectly enclosed, protected, without being
in thrall to the need to express myself. Then I start to talk,
evidently drawing upon some secret reservoir of words and
ideas that must be buried deep inside me, a reservoir that

emerges every time I need it, that's never betrayed me, and the day that it fails to come to my rescue it'll be time for me to start thinking of a new line of work, if you can call this work.

That day, completely off topic with respect to the game theory that the mathematicians had talked about and the fine literary lecture by Richard Ford, I started telling the audience about what had been crushing my spirit for years: the empty discouragement that I'd seen stretching over my people and my city, the unstoppable decline of ambition, the abandonment of the most fragile and naive yet vital dreams, the immoral spread of the awareness that the future was bound to be worse than the present.

As I was venting my despair, I noticed that those formidable middle-aged Milanese, the finest audience of all, were beginning to recover from the interminable lecture interlarded with lukewarm one-liners Odifreddi had hammered at them. They looked up at me with renewed interest, and every now and again they exchanged gestures of approval. They nodded, they elbowed one another. They flashed bitter smiles—someone even applauded, briefly—as I recounted the exploits of Sergio Vari in boomtown Milan, at the height of the export fever, and like a bolt from the blue it came to me that they might actually be interested in the story I was telling them. It was at that moment, I believe, that I decided to write this book—and as the exultation of the undertaking was just on the verge of choking off the words in my mouth, I decided to end my talk with a question directed at Richard Ford. I asked him what *he* thought of the iron grip that the laws of the marketplace were now exerting, after spoiling us for decades, on the Italy of small manufacturers and artisans, on my city, on me, and on my people, and *what we ought to do about it.*

You might consider that a naive, out-of-place question, the SOS of a fishing trawler to an ocean liner on a raging stormy sea, but I know that there are writers capable of seeing the things of this world even before they happen, and I wanted the opinion of someone who knows so much about life that he is able to endow with greatness even the life of a New England real estate salesman. I wanted an answer from the great bard of normalcy, the novelist who has one of his characters say, in *The Sportswriter,* "Do you think it's too little to do with your life? Just collect tolls, raise a family, work on an old car like this, go out on the ocean with your son and fish for fluke? Maybe love your wife?"

I wanted an answer from Raymond Carver's friend.

Ford immediately replied that he didn't know, he couldn't say, and perhaps no one could give an answer to my question, and he started a long series of observations about the things he didn't like about George Bush's America, but from the way he kept turning to look at me as he spoke, I understood that he had liked the question, and that he wasn't satisfied with the answer he had given me.

At the end of his response, Richard turned to look at me, leveling his wolven gray eyes on mine, and he said this formidable phrase: "Still, Edoardo, I'm sure that in the end, somehow, *the economy will succumb to an act of the imagination.*"

Losing Money
Through a Firehose

Since we sold the company, I've had nothing more to do with business, and I've done my best to make my living as a writer.

In October 2004, a few days after selling the company, my fifth novel, *L'età dell'oro* (The Golden Age), was published. In it I told the life story of an imaginary Prato textiles entrepreneur, now in his seventies, Ivo Barrocciai, who had gone bankrupt and lost everything as a result of a crisis that had devastated the Prato textile industry and small-scale Italian industry as a whole, which finally succumbed to the suffocating grip of globalization. The story was set in 2010, that is to say, the present. I thought frequently about how I'd manage to keep working in the company after the publication of *L'età dell'oro*: surely, I wouldn't be able to. Maybe it was fate that this novel should accompany me to the end of my career as an industrialist and serve as the baptism for a new career.

In 2005 I was nominated for the Strega Prize. Or perhaps *L'età dell'oro* was nominated, I've never really understood how it works. Everyone told me, from the very outset, that I wouldn't win. This was the year when Maurizio Maggiani would win the Strega—it even said so in the newspapers. And in fact, Maggiani won.

I won only the first vote, the one that takes place in Rome in Casa Bellonci and serves to reduce the number of competitors from twelve to five, in a happy, tangled evening, painful and stunning, which I spent on that magical terrace drinking white wine and looking down on the same roofs of Rome that Moravia and Buzzati had looked out on, all alone because my wife Carlotta was at the hospital in Arezzo at the bedside of her ailing father, Sergio Carpini.

Carpini fought like a lion and then passed away on Christmas Eve 2006, leaving me a dozen or so yellowed notebooks from the 1950s in which, right after graduating from technical school, he made notes on the weaves of his first overcoat design patterns, a torrent of ideas and colors and combinations that nowadays would generate a burst of applause from the idiots that cluster around the runways of the fashion shows and truly believe that fashion springs always and exclusively from a *designer's creativity*. The same Carpini who in the seventies felt he had the right to perform alchemy with fabrics, and who washed the finest cashmere fabrics in industrial washing machines, boiled silk, mixed wool with linen, and with his own hands wove certain spectacular silk and linen design patterns that he dyed in his beloved strong colors, in stripes and checks and weaves and patterns that had never been seen before but that since then you've seen a thousand times, being worn by beautiful actresses, in the fantastic movies of those years. The same Carpini who was mentor and wet nurse to many of the designers you now know, the ones who may now have billion-dollar empires, but who, back then when they were young, showed up humbly in the weaving mill to see the collection. He would spend entire afternoons with them and then invite them to dinner in the big house in the hills where I now live, and by the light of the setting sun he would show them, proud and truth-twistingly boastful, the vista of industrial sheds stretching out to the hills of Montalbano and tell them that in Prato, one way or another, everyone worked for him. The same Carpini who one day— fed up at being snubbed at the major textile fairs held at Villa d'Este on Lake Como by the manufacturers from Biella and Como, the exclusive and spectacular fairs where industrialists from Prato weren't welcome due to a mean-spirited Northern apartheid—hired the *Concordia*, an old and wonderfully elegant stern-wheel paddle steamer from the 1920s that on

Saturdays and Sundays carried tourists on excursions around the lake: an extremely luxurious Fascist marvel made of teak with interiors upholstered in red leather—and so he tied the steamboat up at the wharf of Villa d'Este on the first day of the trade fair. The same Carpini who sounded the steamboat's whistle until the clients emerged from the villa, eager to see who was responsible for all that ruckus and, curious as monkeys, trooped down to view his collection and sample bread from Prato and olive oil from La Selva, his estate in the harsh Arezzo Chianti region, and wine from his vineyards and prosciutto and bread soup and the mortadella that Sergio Vari had brought specially for the occasion from Bologna. The same Carpini who decided to sell his company at the end of the eighties, the day a well-known Italian fashion designer first asked him the price of an article—not a discount, the *price*—because, obviously, this amounted in his mind to the end of fashion, it meant that the industry was moving toward a period of great decline. The same Carpini who retired to make wine at La Selva, and there he dreamed of enlarging his little lake by making it overflow onto his land so as to create a true, vast lake, big enough to be featured on maps, a lake where he could land the seaplanes that he dreamed of flying from the pier off Forte dei Marmi to create a convenient link between what he thought of as the two most beautiful places on earth, a link that would permit him to bring to La Selva people who without knowing it had worn clothing made with the fabrics his company had manufactured, those few select individuals who might be capable of appreciating the beauty and pleasure and sybaritic ease that he always talked about without ever explaining what the devil it might be. The same Carpini who had created many of the fabrics used to make the magnificent garments that Carlotta and I saw exhibited as works of art in Palazzo Strozzi, in Florence, in a show of apparel flown over from the permanent collection of the Los Angeles County Museum of Art—and as we were wandering through those Renaissance halls, surrounded by the history of worldwide fashion, Carlotta could even remember and list the names of individual fabrics that her father had invented, and she pointed them out to me one after another, and she had to laugh, bitterly, at the thought that now her daddy was dead and the fabrics, on the other hand, had become *works of art*, and *by other people*, because not even in small print, not even in italics, not even at the bottom of the description, on the elegant museum tags that attributed those wonderful articles of clothing to the designers, was there so much as a mention that those fantastic fabrics had been created by Sergio Carpini, of Prato.

In 2007 my book about Jesus, *Per sempre*, came out, an unassuming and personal novel with a graffitied cover, a book made up of faith found and faith lost, poverty, the Gospels, and cocaine, a book that I still couldn't say to this day where it even came from. Maybe I should never have published it. Maybe I should have just written it—because there is no question that I *needed* to write it—and kept it to myself, locked in a safe, like something Salinger would do, and only let the people I like and trust read it, this strange book that I'll never be able to forget because I had the title tattooed over my heart. When someone asks me why, I usually answer that it's just a tattoo, that there are no major hidden explanations: I just liked those two words, that's all.

But that's not really true, it's not that simple.

Most important, that's not the way it is.

Per sempre—forever, for always—is a way of saying that at age forty-eight I finally realized that memories are the cost of living; that any and all ties with my youth now depend upon memory, and memory alone, the implacable monster that refuses to be silenced; that there are things and people and events and lacerating loves and pains and joys that I'll never be able to forget, that will stay with me, in fact, *for always*; that the blackboard of my life, in other words, cannot be erased, and every new thing that may come into my mind to write on it will have to find room, wedged into the few remaining empty spaces.

These are the experiences and the disappointments of my first five years as a writer, during which I did nothing other than write and read and worry about how I'd be able to live without doing anything other than write and read, terrified at the idea of sliding into poverty and tormented by the saying my grandmother Flora used to recite: *Dig away and never add, even a great mountain will wear away,* until it finally dawned on me that in the last few years of pure economic folly it was precisely *doing nothing entrepreneurial* that proved to be the soundest entrepreneurial strategy available. Any company I might have founded over the last five years would certainly be on the brink of disaster by now. If I had listened to the advice of those who urged me to start a new textile company, set up a winery in Chianti, build or buy apartments in Miami and Montevarchi, start a contemporary art gallery, or design a line of apparel, in all likelihood I would have lost money through a firehose. I could have tried working in publishing, maybe I could even have founded a publishing house all my own, but by now it's become clear to me that the books I like tend to find favor with few other people, although the few that do like them love them intensely, and these books become best sellers only if the author dramatically takes his life.

I lived on what I had, and I wrote as much as I was able. I determined to bring every day to an end by doing my best to be happy, telling myself over and over that it is a great privilege to be able to live without working, that many people I know would gladly trade places with me, that I'm a very, very fortunate man.

But how long can this go on?

That Gold Dust

My father signs first, followed by Alvaro.

The notary D'Ambrosi gathers up the papers that constitute the legal document, gets to his feet, bids us all farewell, and leaves the conference room. For us, the time has come when we promise to see each other more often, to have dinner out, all of us together, with our wives, to deplore the fact that we see so little of each other anymore. We slowly don our coats, and Alvaro compliments me on my knickerbocker overcoat. He asks me whether it cost more or less than five hundred euros retail. When I tell him that I bought it used and that I paid thirty euros for it he breaks out laughing and tells my father that I resemble no Nesi before me. We file out of the notary's office. First my father,

then Alvaro, then me. We ride down in silence in the eleva-
tor until we reach the ground floor. More feeble farewells,
more promises we'll never keep, more meager smiles. Someone suggests that we go get a cup of coffee together, but the
idea is aborted immediately and, after a few more awkward
seconds, Alvaro says goodbye and heads off toward his car.
My father and I stand there for a moment in silence, then
he tells me that he needs to have a dead pine taken down on
his property and asks me to give him the phone number of
Yari, my titanic gardener friend who's a death metal fan and
the singer in a rock group he founded: Clitorideath.

I adore my father. In 2008 I had his name tattooed on
my left forearm: ALVARADO. Before having it tattooed, I asked
him permission: in other words, whether he was happy to
have me tattoo his name in such a prominent location. He
told me that he would be *honored*.

Ever since he first learned to text, four years ago, and fell
in love with this new technology, scarcely a day goes by that
we don't write each other, often to tell each other things that
we'd never say face to face, either because they're too portentous or too frivolous. I believe he likes the fact that texting
allows him to communicate freely, without the implicit de-
nuding of self that comes of speaking to someone in the flesh,
and that he feels absolved by the transitory nature of texting;
he takes care not to save any text message for more than a day
or two, no matter what its content. I'm deeply comforted by

this concise, detailed way of staying in touch with him even without seeing him, and I'm amused by the idea of using such a modern and perfect means of communication, which often has more in common with telepathy than with telephony, with my seventy-seven-year-old father.

And so, when I find the gardener's number on my cell phone, my father asks me to text it to him, says goodbye, turns, and heads over to his white car. A careful, three-point turn, the xenon headlights, which he always turns on when the morning is dull and gray, sweep their beam across me, then with a quick wave of the hand he's already vanished from sight. I'm left there alone, clutching a copy of the document that we've just signed in one hand, and my head rings with the words that Fitzgerald wrote about New York in 1932, in the midst of the Great Depression: "Thus I take leave of my lost city . . . it no longer whispers of fantastic success and eternal youth . . . All is lost save memory."

It's the leaden morning of one of those days when writing is impossible, editing what I've written is dangerous, and even reading is inadvisable. One of those days when my memory brings me the bill and *everything* reminds me of my past, and I'm obtuse and depressed and I have nothing to say to anyone and nothing on my mind, and all I seem able to do is drive aimlessly through the streets of my city, along with and alongside other cars, so many fish all swimming in the same school.

The other drivers are all absorbed in phone calls: some of them are declaiming and gesticulating—and I imagine, or rather I hope, that what they're doing is shouting into the dashboard microphones of their hands-free car phones—but most of them mulishly insist on driving along with their neck twisted to clamp the cell phone between ear and shoulder, and you can't help but be afraid of these lines of hunchbacks who often lurch suddenly out of their lanes, though now without triggering those furious, indignant choruses of horns that were such common accompaniments in my youth, when the quality of one's driving was considered to be a faithful reflection of the intellectual capacity of the driver and every negative comment on one's driving became a personal insult, to the point that it was common to get into fights over issues of *the rules of the road* and there were fistfights over a failure to respect a stop sign or even over an awkwardly parked car.

Nowadays, in contrast, everyone fumbles around in a total eclipse of attention—and I'm no better than the rest of them, because as a pioneer and an advocate of the automatic transmission from the earliest days, back when it was looked upon with scorn and contempt and considered to be roughly analogous to those specialized command consoles that allow paraplegics and amputees to drive cars, I can afford to be the most distracted driver of all, since I don't even have to shift gears, and so I increasingly find myself lost in a reverie for long minutes at a time, driving through the farmland and countryside that surround my city, steering down narrow country roads that threaten any minute to turn into dusty white dirt lanes, traveling toward towns that I've never even heard of before, towns that don't even show up on the screen of the GPS navigator, where the little arrow that stands for my car is lost against a gray background of nothingness.

This morning, though, I know where I want to go. It's going to be a short and painful journey, along roads that I know well, far too well—and since it's a journey toward silence, I listen to music as I drive, even though I don't really know anything about music. I can't tell one note from another, in fact I don't really even know what a note is. I don't know and I've never understood why there are seven notes—as opposed to nine notes, for instance, or twelve, or forty-six. I know the terms *adagio* and *allegro*, but aside from my appreciation for the velvety sound of these fine old names, I couldn't say what they mean if my life depended on it. The same is true of the *tone* and the *color* of music, even of *harmony*. All of them abstractions that I pretend to understand. I know that there's such a thing as *counterpoint*, but I don't know what it is. The things I like in music are the names: *harpsichord, oboe, double bass. Bassoon* and *contrabassoon. Solfeggio. Xylophone* and *vibraphone. Dodecaphony.*

I have absolutely no ear for music. It is only with the greatest difficulty that I recognize the sound of different instruments and I mangle any song I set out to sing except for "O surdato 'nnammurato," which I perform perfectly and with great confidence because I sang it almost every day back in high school thanks to a close friend who died years ago but who sang it all the time back then.

But I know what I want from music. What I ask of a song, for example, is that it be—or at least that it contain— a narrative. That is, I would like both the music and the lyrics—though I'll settle for it being just one of the two—*to do something*, during the song. Let them increase in intensity, for instance, or let them rise and then empty out. Let them follow a progression, a development of some sort: a before and an after, a beginning and an end. I don't know if that makes sense. I told you before: I don't really know a thing about music. In any case, for the past few weeks I've been listening to a formidable song by Sigur Rós that's more than ten minutes long and is called, I think, "Milano." I'm not sure because on the cover of the album the titles are written in tiny elaborate characters, and in Icelandic, and even though it strikes me as impossible, the more I read the more it looks to me like that's exactly what the song's title is, "Milano," and I refuse to go online to check whether that's right, because in terms of what I want to say it's absolutely irrelevant. The song starts out hushed, quietly, punctuated by silvery notes that seem to be made of crystal, and the volume rises slowly and continuously without the music changing, until the voice comes in, a sort of male falsetto as light as a whisper, serene and grief-laden at the same time, and even though I don't understand Icelandic, I'm sure that he's singing about something very beautiful that has been lost.

As far as I can tell the same words are repeated by that sweet voice as it continues to rise in volume and intensity along with the song, a voice which still manages in some indescribable manner to preserve its aching feeling of being a whisper, and even after it turns into a shout that accompanies the savage and yet exceedingly delicate crescendo, still, it remains a heartfelt shout, deeply human, as if it were somehow really a sigh. Then the song rises to fever pitch and drops back to earth and becomes an instrumental piece again, regaining its serenity, as if it were a lullaby caressed by musical notes of pure crystal.

It's as if it were trying to give me time to catch my breath and regain the heart I had lost, I think to myself. As if some destination had been attained and something important had been stated. As if that incredible heartfelt scream had confided a secret to me. When the miraculous voice comes back, it's little more than a quiver, but it immediately starts weaving its Icelandic enchantment again, and the song resumes its upward ascent, and I'm sure that this wonderful music accompanies the same words and is telling me the same story, only with greater force this time, greater intensity, greater pain.

It's a prayer, that's what it is. A prayer for a memory. I wait for the song to end and I turn off the engine. I've arrived in Narnali, the destination of my journey. I'm parked in front of our weaving mill.

While listening to Sigur Rós I went past the house where Francesco Nuti's mother lives; I used to be friends with him, and I've never met anyone who was so pleased with life as he was—Francesco, who hired me as an assistant director for one of his movies, and who asked me to find a way to turn Piazza Santa Croce white as if it had just snowed and—no sooner said than done—I ordered three truckloads of rock salt and I turned all Piazza Santa Croce white, and when you walked on that salt, even though it was the middle of August, as God is my witness you shivered from the cold; Francesco, who, ever since he had his damned accident, I've lacked the courage to go and see, coward that I am; Francesco, who is there, at his mother's house, slowly recuperating, and I send him warm thoughts, and I beg his forgiveness.

Not fifty yards from Francesco's mother's house, on the same road, Via Ortigara, is the company, *our* company, the Lanificio T.O. Nesi & Figli S.p.A., where I haven't set foot once since the day we sold the business. I always do my best not to look in through the open front door as I drive by, but it's the rare day I succeed. I almost always take a glance, as I do today. Out front, there are cars and trucks parked in a line. Apparently, they manage to go on working, even without me.

I get out of my car and I see that the notary was right when he wrote in the legal document that the industrial shed that houses the weaving mill has no street number. There is, in fact, no number in sight, anywhere. We worked for more than forty years in an industrial shed that was *our property*, down at the end of a city street, not three hundred yards from the Narnali church, and no one ever bothered to request that the place be assigned a street number. I sigh, unlock the old rusty gate, push it open, and, after twenty paces, no more, I come to the large closed door. In a corner the wind has piled up paper, trash, a sheet of newspaper, a flier from a pizzeria. I slide the key into the lock, pull open the door, and a wall of silence pours out over me: a new silence, harsh and powerful as a punch in the jaw, the silence that I've come here to listen to.

If you've never walked into an operating weaving mill you can really have no idea of the level of noise it generates. The noise of a weaving mill is something dense, practically a solid mass. It's a wave that crashes over you, a wind that makes you hunch over. The noise of a weaving mill makes you half close your eyes and smile; it's like running through falling snow. The noise of a weaving mill makes you hold your breath, the way a newborn does when you blow in its face. The noise of a weaving mill is continuous and inhuman, made up of thousands of overlapping metallic sounds, and yet there are times when it seems like laughter. The noise of a weaving mill has no clear point of origin and seems to come out of the ground or the air, because seen from a distance the looms appear to be motionless. The noise of a weaving mill reaches and often climbs past ninety decibels, and it befuddles and deafens those who fail to put earplugs in their ears: it's like the sirens' song that tormented Ulysses. The noise of a weaving mill resembles the clangor of a vast army marching straight at you, the buzz of a gigantic beehive. At times, if it's very far away, you can mistake it for the rumble of a thunderstorm. The noise of a weaving mill never stops, and it's the most venerable and ancient song of our city, and to the children of Prato it serves as a lullaby.

We Nesis have been forced to silence it, this weaving mill of ours. We shut it down this very morning. We called it Ines, and it took its name, befitting a grande dame, from an anagram of our surname—a two-bit trick, though it never failed to impress our suppliers and bankers. They always assumed that I had named it, that it was just one more of the arrogant, creative names of the Nesis, perhaps a literary reference of some kind, possibly a reference to some heroine out of Tolstoy—but instead it was much more. It was another version of our name, and therefore another version of us, and it was Alvaro who first came up with it, perhaps to make me remember that the weaving mill had been the incubator of our grandparents' dreams, that it had been our first stepping-stone to the world of the textile industry in the 1920s, when Mussolini was in charge and women couldn't vote and the world of the people of Prato ended in Florence.

We paid off everyone, the workers and our suppliers and the tax collectors, and we shut down the weaving mill. In a few days, we'll sell off the looms. They'll be shipped to India, I think, or to Sri Lanka, or Pakistan. I don't know where and I don't want to know. After selling off the wool mill—the Lanificio—Ines (that's what I always called it, without the article: never *L'Ines*) went on working for an array of reasons that weren't entirely rational, and over the past four years it was under a form of administration that was singular, to say the least, and—here we can apply the term—distinctly literary. We had a single client, thirteen looms, and five employees. We charged fairly good prices, but they were never high enough to actually make a substantial profit, and so every year the balance sheet wavered between a small profit and a small loss. Basically, Ines was breaking even.

The singular and literary thing is that, in order to break even, Ines neither paid rent to the owner of the industrial shed, which was us, nor did the mill pay a salary to management, which was us again. The invoices our sole client paid went straight to covering the electric bills, production costs, upkeep and maintenance on the machinery, a limited amortization fund, the accountant who kept the books, the tax lawyers, and the workers themselves. And, of course, the IRAP imposed by the Honorable Vincenzo Visco— hallowed be his name.

The unintended implementation of the core principles of Soviet Communist statism through Ines was not approved at the drawing table by the board of directors, which by the way is made up of a team of old free-market laissez-faire capitalists; rather it became necessary with the almost daily rise in structural costs and the corresponding contraction of profits, until there remained only one tacit tactic to keep from closing down the weaving mill entirely—which was the one thing we were unwilling to do, come what may. That is what led to the latest and most peculiar of the countless incarnations of the Prato businessman: the nonprofit entrepreneur.

We had invented a comical, bittersweet entrepreneurial volunteerism and, like something straight out of Jonathan Swift, there were days when I amused myself by imagining a distant land with a name consisting mostly of consonants that resolved the problems arising from its economic downturn by summoning out of retirement brigades of bored ex-industrialists sick of doing nothing all day and putting them in charge of troubled companies with too many employees who would be too expensive in terms of social costs to lay off. The companies would benefit from the retirees' decades of experience and skill without having to pay them a cent, because the elderly entrepreneurs would happily work free of charge, as long as they didn't have to stay home watching television and arguing with their wives about lunch, dinner, and where to put the knickknacks in the living room.

Relaxed and untroubled, without pressure, freed of the burden of ownership and the weight of ambition, the re-tired industrialists would finally be able to have fun at work without being slaves to the duty to earn money, and their only responsibility would be to keep the company afloat, just earning enough to keep paying the employees' salaries and withholding costs, as well as IRAP—because they also would have IRAP in that Swiftian land with a name made up mostly of consonants.

It was a fucked-up form of amusement, no question, and my laughter was forced and harsh, like the sound of a laughing hyena, because it was obvious, so to speak, that Ines kept its head above water only because it stood tiptoed on the shoulders of giants, and there was no way for us to forget that there had been a time when those giants were us. I measure off the shed with small paces, I brush past the looms, I blow away the fluffy fuzz of the wool and the still dustier mantle of cotton residue that seems to have settled on everything. I caress the remaining ends of the cut bolts of cloth, and I even manage to guess the name of certain of the fabrics. I listen to this new heavy silence, broken only by the chirping of small birds that must have made their way in through a broken window somewhere and nested inside Ines. I wonder whether those birds were already in here before, while the looms were clattering away day and night, and whether a bird can go deaf. I walk along the rows of looms illuminated by a chilly light that filters through at an angle from the large skylight windows in the barrel-vault roof and I decide that they're beautiful. I could take them to the Venice Biennale exactly as they are, with the fuzz on the temples and the cut canvases and the black fingermarks of the head weaver Ciabatti, and set them up in one of the immense sheds of the Arsenale, with the inevitable title, *Untitled*, and they'd immediately become works of art.

Maybe I just never really understood what was happening, in all these years, in our cavernous industrial shed without a street number. What was created, in here, now that it's gone? Who were all those people who worked at the looms with the metaphysical objective of making them run constantly, day and night, and where are they now, and what do they recall of the endless days spent working for me and my family?

Maybe I just never really understood what work is. Maybe I just used other people's work—the same way I used my own work. Maybe I just used my own life, instead of living it.

Why did I always sense decadence around me, even when it wasn't there? Why, ever since I was little, did I think and fear and *know* that everything—*everything*—would come to an end? Why are my heroes the ones who live amidst ruins? Why have I always rooted for Hector and not for Achilles, for Sparta and not for Athens, for the Carthaginians and not for the Romans?

Suddenly a shaft of sunlight that has escaped from the blanket of leaden clouds overhead penetrates through the big windows, dazzling me, and I see stars dancing on the screen of my eyelids and I'm reminded of the words of Booth Tarkington in *The Magnificent Ambersons*, the second and last novel I decided to publish during my exceedingly brief interregnum as the editorial director of Fandango Libri: "It seems to me the gold-dust he thinks was here is just his being young that he remembers," and I can feel that infernal mechanism as it starts grinding away inside of me, a clockwork I can't seem to defuse, and which I've learned to dread, a mechanism that demands that every single thing remind me of something else, in a chain reaction of comprehensions whose beginning I can glimpse but whose ultimate end is unknown and unknowable, and the one thing I can rest assured of is that it will pursue a twisting, turning path and will take me on a journey that won't always be enjoyable, a journey that more closely resembles a frantic trip on a roller coaster than an excursion in a horse-drawn carriage.

And now two marvelous scenes appear before my eyes, scenes from the film that Orson Welles stubbornly insisted on basing on the novel. The first is the grand Amberson ball, when the camera moves as if it's floating on air in the wonderfully reconstructed rooms of their wonderful castle-home, and in a single, incredibly long take without a single cut, manages to recount and portray the magnificence of an era. The second is the lovely sequence of the initial narrative, which depicts a world of lost gentility, where if a lady whistled when the streetcar was approaching, the streetcar would halt at once to wait for her while she shut the window, put on her hat and coat, went downstairs, and told the girl what to have for dinner before boarding the car—and none of the other passengers would ever think of objecting.

But it already seems to be time to start off on my involuntary trip again, and so I recall the memorable story of the destruction of that film and the simultaneous destruction of Welles himself: of how the director, who, immediately after he finished shooting the film about the Ambersons, madly flew off to Brazil to make another movie about Carnaval in Rio and remained there, unable to travel because of the war, and supervised the editing through interminable telegrams to his assistant, while the producers, terrified by the disastrous results of the first public screening, shown to an audience too young to appreciate it, hired a herd of rank beginners to trim and clip and manipulate and remix

The Magnificent Ambersons with insipid new scenes, until they had completely distorted its true nature, turning a deaf ear to the further, despairing Lowryesque telegrams in which Welles indicated all the cuts and modifications to be made to the film, which finally came out in the version approved by the rank beginners and was so unsuccessful that the producer was fired and Orson Welles—the young prodigy who had invented live radio with *The War of the Worlds* and whose first film as a director was *Citizen Kane*—turned into *that guy who wants to make art films but never finishes them*, and he eventually became what was destined to be his sempiternal icon, the gigantic defeated lonely man whom Ed Wood meets in a Los Angeles bar, in the middle of the afternoon, in Tim Burton's film of that name.

Peter Bogdanovich tells us that, even though Welles had always claimed to have simply refused to see his movie about the Ambersons, at least one time he definitely did watch it, on television, in a bungalow at the Beverly Hills Hotel where he lived with the beautiful Croatian actress Oja Kodar.

He watched his poor ravaged movie, Orson Welles did, squatting in front of the screen like a soccer player in the old pictures in fan magazines, because he couldn't stand to see it and he couldn't stand not to see it, and he wept in silence, his back turned to his companion and his friends to keep them from seeing him. When Bogdanovich, a few days later, gathered the courage to ask him what effect see-ing the movie after all these years had had on him, Welles gave him an answer that shot an enchanted arrow into the air that flew over land and sea for decades and decades only to strike me square in the heart, today, as I stand frozen in the middle of the industrial shed that houses my inactive, sold-off weaving mill, in Narnali, with my soul in confusion and a knickerbocker overcoat and my memory overflowing with an Icelandic rock song and my eyes shut to keep from being blinded by the winter sunshine.

What Orson Welles said to his friend Bogdanovich was: "Well, I was upset, but not because of the cutting. That just makes me furious. Don't you see? It was because it's the *past.* It's *over.*"

Immediately

You showed up and rang the front doorbell, and they immediately opened the door to you. They immediately let you into the darker recesses of this filthy old decaying industrial shed, with its grayish plastered walls, the scratched linoleum flooring, flaking and patched, the air stale with smoke and breath. An industrial shed divided in two by plasterboard partition walls, filthy and collapsing, brightly lit up by fluorescent tubes dangling from the ceiling, crudely wired to black cables as thick as fingers that cluster into bundles the size of pythons and snake along on plastic platforms that loom off-kilter above rows of brand-new sewing machines that are somehow already filthy, besieged by half-open cartons, scraps of fabric of all colors, ashtrays overflowing with stubbed-out butts, cans of Red Bull crushed in anger and half-empty bottles of water.

You're the state police, you're the firemen, you're the city constables, you're the local health department. You are traveling in your own city, but it's actually the city of the Chinese. Next to you, the last in a line of twenty-year-olds, a young man, motionless, eyes glistening, hunches his diminutive shoulders inside a short-sleeve, pea-green knit shirt, with TONY MONTANA printed on the back in gothic letters. He's wearing slim, dark jeans, decorated with gilt stripes that run down his skinny legs, thin as chopsticks, and a pair of phosphorescent Nikes. There's just a haze of whiskers on his face, and smooth, raven-black hair, short and stiff on top of his head, long and lank, dangling over his ears, in a bizarre and vaguely canine hairstyle unlike anything you've ever seen before. He's had his hands in his pockets the whole time since you came in. He doesn't know a word of Italian. He won't look at you, he won't look at anyone, with his glazed, glistening eyes. His gaze is fixed on the floor, staring down into the void, and he complies immediately when the policeman walks over to him and gestures to him to spread his arms so he can be searched, but with the first cautious palpations, he starts to look over at his friends and he smiles, and you feel a strange sense of relief. His eyes aren't glazed, then, after all. He just has the watery eyes of so many young men his age. He's not upset, he's not despairing. He's not about to cry. And why should he, for that matter?

Nothing's happening, and they all know it. You are the one who does not know. You, who would fall to your knees in tears if the police raided your business and put judicial seals everywhere, confiscating your industrial shed and your company, if by some chance you still owned them. You, who are on the verge of tears just at the sight of this happening to other people. You, who don't understand, who may be unable to understand.

There might be twenty or so of them, though it's hard to say the exact number. Aside from the five or six young men and women lined up, the others keep walking silently into and out of the little cubicles marked out with plasterboard, moving with bowed heads through the corridors of this ant colony. They were sewing what look like pinafores for newborns, but you can't tell for sure that that's what they are. They're fairly small pieces of cloth, made of pink cotton. They could be blouses, skirts, pajamas. They could be doll clothes.

The oldest Chinese man might be forty or so. He hasn't even budged from his workplace at the sewing machine, and he's smoking with slow gestures. A woman is trying without success to understand what the fire chief is saying to her, she slowly shakes her head, she shrugs her shoulders. Two beautiful children in undershirts chase each another around and between the sewing machines, pedaling colorful plastic tricycles, ignored by one and all, and they carry on a cheerful, noisy conversation that never ceases for an instant throughout the entire visit, if that's what we want to call this. A young woman walks up dressed in pajamas, a towel tossed over one shoulder as if she were a boxer's second, and she surveys the scene, her eyes still buttoned up with sleep. We woke her up, even though this is the most mild-mannered police raid in the history of the world.

The two owners—because the industrial shed has been divided in two by drywall partitions separating two different companies—willingly give their details to the policemen and firemen. They can't be much older than twenty, the owners: they're just kids and they reply courteously in monosyllables, smiling, to the questions that are put to them. They give the impression of knowing how to speak Italian much better than you'd guess from their bitten-off words. At a certain point there's an impasse concerning the number of sweatshop workers, and the interpreter is summoned, a tall Chinese man with a quiff and a Lacoste, who explains at considerable length the questions that the policemen and firemen are asking, speaking in their syncopated language, but he only obtains from the owners very short and apparently incomplete answers, because he keeps shaking his head.

And you call this working?

Cruel and derisive is the economic brain twister according to which, while the Prato economic district and all of the Italian textile industry have long since plunged into what may be an irreversible crisis caused by the unfettered worldwide importation of Chinese fabrics, it is right here in Prato, in industrial sheds left empty by the tiny companies that have gone bankrupt, sheds that are often built within the city limits, next to the homes of the owners, in compliance with the age-old notion that your life is your work and your work is your life, it is here that one of the largest Chinese communities in all Europe has sprung up, a community that lives and prospers by giving work to illegal immigrants and sewing garments with fabrics that they *import from China*, because the fabrics that the Pratese mills make are too expensive, but they still therefore have every right to label their rags Made in Italy.

It starts to get hot, and you perspire. All the windows are closed, to make sure that no one can look in from outside. In the barrel roof of the industrial shed, way up high, there's a sort of porthole and through it you can see a single star twinkling, ridiculously alone.

The fire chief comes over and shows you the eight empty propane canisters scattered throughout the warehouse. He tells you that they're almost more dangerous than full ones, because of the *risk of explosion*. He shows you the fire extinguishers, recently checked out and overhauled, but since tossed into a corner and buried under scraps of fabric. He takes you to see the jury-rigged kitchen, a hotplate connected to a propane canister in a way that makes even you shiver in horror. He shows you bare electric wires, running everywhere.

"Go see where they sleep," the fire chief tells you. "*Get the whole picture.*"

You do your best to remind yourself that this isn't someone's house: it's an illegal warehouse that's about to be shut down and sealed and confiscated, it's *material evidence*, and so there's nothing wrong with you walking into bedrooms that aren't bedrooms, into hallways that aren't hallways, into common rooms that aren't common rooms, if you look at the imitation of life and work that is rehearsed every day in your city in hundreds of industrial sheds just like this one.

You tell yourself that you're not nosy, you're not prying. Damn it, you came here with the police, and you're a writer. You're here to tell the world what you see and hear. You're serving a purpose, whether or not you want to, whether or not you believe in it, and so you move away from Ceccato's side, from your friend from the local ASL, or health authority, who goes on making notes of code violations and zoning infractions. You brush past a town constable who's starting the job of putting judicial seals on all the sewing machines. You wander through the industrial shed, your heart sinking in your chest with the weight of a stone.

Separated from the big room with the sewing machines by the same drywall partitions as elsewhere is a series of cubicles in which these young men and women evidently rest between one shift and the next. You take a look from the threshold because, even though there's no door, you're ashamed to go in. All the same, you see the mattresses tossed on the floor, the squalid pallets, the balled-up linen, the pillows still hollowed out by the weight of the heads that have rested on them—all those rags tossed wholesale onto the bed or piled up on filthy shelves that are nothing more than a plea for privacy, an unutterably poor simulacrum of property, of home.

It's unbelievable how many computers there are in this rabbit warren. They must seem to these people like their only link with their homeland, with their infinitely distant loved ones, and you can imagine them weeping as they read an e-mail, the Chinese of Prato, heads cradled in their hands, bone weary from work that never seems to end, as they reply with empty promises to those who most suffer from their absence, victims of the infernal deception of technology that simulates the presence of your nearest and dearest to the point of making you feel that they're right there with you, but they're not, and when you finally manage to glimpse them on a screen, they're a few inches tall, and their voices gouge holes into your heart no matter what they say, because you're so far away.

How could you help but identify with them? How could you fail to think of times when you've been far from home? How can you fail to pity them?

Everything is filthy, horribly filthy. The floors, the sewing machines, the windowless airless cubicles with their pallets and cots are all foul. The blankets are foul, the bathrooms are foul. Everything is horribly neglected, as if it were impossible to clean what would only begin to get dirty again, as if the idea of considering this vast mess to be a home were madness, ridiculous, beautifying what can never be beautified. It seems that they have decided that this is a time to hang tough, and nothing more. A time to hold out against the suffocating heat, even in springtime, and the dank biting chill in the winter, against the windows that they can't open, for fear someone might see them. To hold out against fatigue and sleepiness, and to sleep and eat when they can, and grit their teeth and never stop dreaming and hoping that thanks to their stubborn mulish resistance they may someday be able to leave here, rich perhaps, and still young.

A policeman is asking a young woman with frightened eyes to open a large cardboard box. It seems at first glance to be full of canned food, but there's one can that's bigger than all the others, it has a different label, and once it's opened it reveals a fairly strange piece of packaging, white nylon, vacuum-packed. The policeman tells the interpreter to ask the young woman what it is, and her eyes get bigger and she responds with a certain excitement. The interpreter translates: "It's against inflammations, because she suffers a great deal from inflammations."

Then the policeman asks, "Yes, but what is it?"

So the girl tears open the white vacuum-packed wrapping and displays what's inside: a number of white strips. She puts a handful of them into her mouth, mumbles something, and the interpreter translates: "It's made from animal horn."

The policeman stares at her as she chews and swallows, then he turns to look at you, doubtfully, and asks, "It looks like paper to me, what do you think?"

You look at him and you don't know what to say because it's true, he's right. They seem like so many strips of paper, whatever it is that the Chinese girl is chewing as she looks us in the eyes and smiles. She nods, grabs two handfuls, and offers them to the policemen and to me.

"Try it," she tells us. "It's good for you."

Prato is a city of wicked questions and wicked thoughts.

Prato takes you by the scruff of your neck and shoves your nose into the piss, the way old men used to do to dogs that had shit where they shouldn't. Even the most powerful words, the most elevated concepts seem to be emptied of meaning in the face of this horrendous story of indifference and exploitation among losers, where all the characters are victims of a chain of dishonesty that spreads out from a deeply rotten idea of work.

In Prato today, legality and law, immigration, tolerance and intolerance, ideology, acceptance, racism, and integration, xenophobia, and inclusiveness all turn into so much rusty old junk incapable of helping us to understand what's happening in a city under invasion by a silent and frightened army that so many people here are afraid is nothing but the vanguard of a much larger invasion still to come, but which even now is already impossible to survey or count or stop with spot checks and random raids and the querulous ordinances issued by mayors and the citations issued by firemen and the legal confiscation of the industrial sheds and the covering up of the signs in Chinese and the plastic seals and white-and-red crime scene tape and the Viro padlocks. It's an astonishingly young army of extortion victims who often fail to recognize the depth of the inadequacy of their working conditions and who are content to live and work the way they live and work, walled up inside filthy industrial sheds like this one, because in the heart of China where they come from, they were much, much worse off, and the luckiest ones earned eight dollars a month.

And yet, how are we supposed to live side by side with such widespread and glaring criminal behavior, practiced by thousands of people, all members of a single ethnic group, who show total disregard for our system of law—that is, when they are even aware of it? Should we perhaps begin to feel that it's wrong to consider illegal a phenomenon that is so vast and ubiquitous and apparently unstoppable? Will we wind up framing two separate legal standards, one for the Chinese and one for Italians? Or should we simply begin to treat the Chinese community the way we would treat a community of Finns or Perugians who chose to set up housekeeping in Prato and live there in open violation of our laws, without false pieties or wrongheaded superiority complexes?

But how can we keep from despairing at the growing suspicion that already, in these questions—in these strong and earnest questions that *you* ask—there lurks a treacherous seed of intolerance and racism? Because, of course, it's obvious: as long as these people enter Italy as outlaws, it is as outlaws that they will live here.

And so? What is to be done?

You wander around the industrial shed in a state of shock, your head empty, and you listen as the fire chief patiently goes on explaining to the two owners, little more than children themselves, that fire extinguishers shouldn't be kept buried under piles of scraps of cloth, that they should be mounted somewhere high, where everyone can see them and use them in case there's a fire. You watch the policewoman as she finds yet another empty propane canister right next to one of the cots and she shows it with just a hint of impatience to the owner. You watch Ceccato pointing out a dangling wire to one of the sweatshop workers and explaining that it's dangerous, it's very dangerous, and finally it dawns on you that what you see in their eyes, in the expressions on their faces, in the words and actions of the men and women of the police department, of the firemen, of the city constabulary, of the financial police, of the ASL health authority who came with you into the industrial shed, isn't anger, you don't see contempt, you don't see cold unfriendliness. You don't even see the remote detachment that this sort of spectacle might drive you to adopt.

Instead, what you seem to see is that they are working with something that closely resembles pride, walking tall in the knowledge that they are the last link in a system of values that commands respect and should be fiercely defended, which ultimately takes concrete form in one of the few principles concerning which we all agree in unison, a principle that therefore defines us, we *Westerners*: our adherence to the deep-seated sense of justice that underlies the ideas that helped to shape our body of labor laws, that old and tattered piece of equipment, still gleaming after all these years, a mechanism that was crafted precisely in reaction to the kind of monstrous exploitation of human beings that I see right here before my eyes, a body of laws that is now almost two hundred years old and, albeit far from perfect in any way, for the past two centuries has been slowly but inexorably moving in one direction: to ensure greater rights for people who work, to clearly establish that a right denied remains a right, even if no one protests. And that such a right should be defended. Always.

You ask yourself whether, when it's all said and done, this might not be the gift that twentieth-century Western culture—that immense, irresponsible, cruel, and hilarious madhouse without rhyme or reason in the midst of which you grew up—gives to the world, the ultimate synthesis of everything that it has managed to construct, and you turn your face to the wall because the last thing you want is for them to see you as you choke back a sob, idiot that you are, and you pray inwardly that our people will go on acting in accordance with the heritage of values and the view of the future that took form in the Italian Constitution; that they will never stop trying to understand this hard, adamantine world, this world that's as simple and straightforward as bread, to understand and tolerate, always and forever. Because there is no alternative. The alternative is a nightmare.

By the time you turn around, the raid is over. The depositions have been signed and completed, the sewing machines are under judicial seal. Of the fifteen Chinese workers found in the industrial shed, nine are illegal immigrants, and they will be taken to the police station. The few legal immigrants with valid papers must gather up their belongings, along with the belongings of their illegal compatriots, assemble the children, and march out of the industrial shed before it too is placed under seal. These people will have to find a place to sleep tonight, with their bags in one hand, holding their children by the other, and even if it's a

beautiful spring night, you can't help feeling pity for them.
Believe me, you really can't help it.

You watch the Chinese boy with watery eyes as he is led
into a paddy wagon along with the other eight illegal immigrants, and you wonder how they and the police will be able
to communicate, at police headquarters, since they clearly
don't know a word of Italian. You wonder how any of this
can seem real to them, this life of travel in distant and unfamiliar lands. You wonder if they know where Italy is, where
Florence is, where Prato is. You wonder what they think
of us and our lives and our laws, because, of course, to the
children of the People's Republic of China which had the
best and the brightest of its young people clubbed to death
by illiterate soldiers trucked in to Beijing from Lower Mon-
golia it must seem comical that in Italy the police knock at
the door and stand there waiting for someone to come open
up, that they ascertain the commission of an illegal act and
still no one so much as raises their voice, that they find a
group of illegal immigrants and hand them over to a lukewarm, ineffectual fate: that of being quite simply accompa-
nied downtown to police headquarters and ushered into a
room where a team of policemen will spend hours trying to
determine their names, and once they believe that they have
established their names, those policemen will do nothing
more than put into their hands a sheet of paper written in
a language they do not understand, and then order them

to leave Italy immediately, and then they will let them go, once again free as birds, free to go back to their friends and tell them this incredible story and then fall to the ground laughing and pounding their fists, and then let themselves be locked up once again in another industrial shed to work like donkeys, still in the city of Prato—that is, if they even know that that's the name of this place, this wind-buffeted city of ours.

The Nightmare

The nightmare comes back to me every so often, but never when I'm asleep. It always comes in broad daylight, when I'm in my car, stuck in traffic, and it continues to amass a growing wealth of detail. It's turning into a sort of movie, and this is how it starts: one fall day, in an Italian city, at a self-service gas station, a man is trying to insert a five-euro bill into the slot of an automatic gas pump.

The man is Italian, and he's in his early fifties. He's just been laid off by the company he's worked for since he was twenty-two. His name is Fabio. Fabio's career never really went anywhere. It never really mattered all that much to him. In his eyes, work was always a necessity, never a way to climb the social ladder that he'd always heard about ever since he was a little boy, a ladder however that he has never laid eyes on. He's one of those people who like to say that they work to live, they don't live to work. He has no great loves in his life, with the exception of the Juventus soccer team and American disco music from the 1970s. He's not a slacker or a malingerer. He's a guy who works hard and who does his job, but at five o'clock every day, let the sky fall, he heads home.

He has a family: a wife who works for a bank and two daughters who are the light of his life and who are attending university. One is studying psychology, the other literature. Neither degree is likely to be the surefire path to a job, but he's always insisted that his daughters should study what they care most about. That they pursue something they love. He never had that opportunity himself.

He only had a little less than three years left till he was eligible for retirement, so being laid off was a bitter pill. After thinking it over and examining the situation a thousand times, one morning Fabio finally got up the nerve to go to the owner's office and ask why him, why not someone else, after all these years, and the owner told him how sorry he was, but it didn't change much, the company was going out of business anyway. There were no more orders, no more work, it was all finished. Fabio knew that the man was telling the truth. He worked in the warehouse and he knew for himself how few and how tiny the orders were for the incoming season. He wished he could hate the owner, because it would be a consolation to be able to direct his fury at someone in particular, but he couldn't bring himself to do it. He'd never been able to do it. In fact, he's still absurdly grateful to the man for holding on to his job through the course of two corporate restructurings that followed one on the heels of the other over just a few years. He believed him. The owner had become a defeated lonely old man ever since both his sons refused to come work with him and run the company—now they're both CPAs. There was no bad blood between Fabio and his boss because, in a certain sense, they'd worked together. They were sharing in a certain ineluctability.

Jenny Holzer once said, in one of those very elegant truisms that she put on LEDs in the eighties, "there is a resentment at growing up at the end of an era of plenty," but Fabio would be happy to tell her that there is an even greater resentment at growing old at the end of an era of plenty.

More and more often, he can't seem to get to sleep at night, and he lies awake for hours staring at the ceiling while his wife sleeps peacefully beside him and his mind travels and travels and finally gets lost as it chases after odd thoughts. The strangest thought of them all is turning into a recurring dream. He's in a gigantic empty factory, lit up brightly, and Fabio is surprised and overwhelmed because he's sure that he's in the factory of the world. All around him enormous cogs and toothed gears, oiled and glistening, turn slowly in a counterclockwise direction and transmit their motion to other smaller and still smaller toothed gears, which tick and tick away and vanish into the distance. In the dream Fabio knows that there was a time when the toothed gears were turning in the opposite direction, and that he has to find some way of reversing the rotation because that's the secret, and if he can only do it, everything will go back the way it was and the things that are going wrong now will start going right, the things that are bad now will go back to being good, and so he runs and runs as he searches for the first toothed gear in the factory of the world. He can't find it, but he keeps running and running and searching because he knows that he can't give up. He knows that the only way to change reality is to imagine it as different in a dream, and he knows that if he fails he'll wake up back in his world of dilapidated hopes, and so he runs and runs in the infinite factory. He runs until he wakes up exhausted, and his wife and his daughters have already left the house without making noise and he's alone in the house, it's late morning, and he has nothing to do.

For two weeks now Fabio has been looking for another job. He's a warehouseman, he manages leftover stock, and as far as he's concerned it makes no difference whether the leftover stock is bolts of cloth or computers or ceramic tiles. He could easily do his job in any business that has a warehouse, but nobody seems to even want to have a warehouse full of merchandise that they might or might not be able to sell anymore, and no one seems to have any need of him either, even though, since he's in *mobilità*,* the company that hired him wouldn't have to pay for any of his benefits—no social security, no health insurance. Apparently, however, there are plenty of other people in *mobilità*. It seems as if everyone is in *mobilità*. And he's in his fifties.

The very first few days weren't really all that bad. It was as if he had rediscovered some kind of freedom, and he started taking long walks through the center of town. He inhaled the brisk cool morning air, he looked around at other people, he looked at shop windows. He sat on benches and admired for thirty minutes at a time the endlessly changing spectacle of the sky, astonished at the beauty of the sight. For the very first few days he told himself that it wasn't his fault that he'd been laid off, that there was much more to life than work, and that he needed to make an effort to see things in those terms. There were even times when he had cherished the thought that there was still a lot he could do with his life, he'd fostered the illusion that he could rely on himself and his own strength. After all, he wasn't old, he told himself. He wasn't an imbecile. He wasn't a loser.

---

*An Italian social welfare provision whereby the state pays a laid-off person part of his previous salary for three years.

On his fifth morning walk, however, he realized that he'd already seen everything there was to see in the center of his town: that he knew the shop windows all by heart, the colors of the buildings, even the gaps between the cobblestones in the street. Because, of course, he'd stopped looking up at the sky. He tried spending time in bars. He liked reading newspapers. Before, he'd almost never had the time or the interest. He started reading the papers from the front page to the back. He started commenting on the articles, at first under his breath and before long out loud, but when he tried to talk with the other customers in the bar, he realized that he was no longer capable of keeping up with their conversations, not even on the subject of soccer. His opinions seemed to be as light as feathers. He decided to stop walking through the city—he'd developed blisters on his feet. That spelled the end of his rediscovery of freedom.

Every day is becoming longer, more challenging.

Fabio begins to feel ashamed at being out of work, and he can't stand staying home. He even feels guilty about sitting on the sofa and watching TV in the evening, because, having done nothing all day long, he has nothing to rest from. And yet he's exhausted—and depressed. He's become anxious. He snaps at the slightest provocation. He shouts a lot, and he never used to shout at all. He stays out of the house all day, even though he has nothing to do. He measures his day against lunchtime and dinnertime, but there's no one home at lunchtime because his daughters are off somewhere studying and his wife eats a salad at the café next to the bank, and at dinner he has to deal with how painful it is to encounter the gazes of his women, their silences, and then the long, terrible evening begins, stretched out on the sofa, watching television by himself because his daughters and wife always have something else to do. Something, anything, as long as they don't have to watch television with him, because by now all he ever wants to watch are programs that talk about how the economy is going from bad to worse.

This is his new life of unemployment, like it or not. He starts driving around the city in his almost new car, a Fiat Grande Punto that runs on gas instead of the cheaper diesel, purchased foolishly just two years ago, when the idea of being laid off seemed to belong to the realm of the impossible. The installments on the car seem to stretch out to infinity. He paid far too much for it, that stupid car. It even has air-conditioning. Sometimes, when he feels bad, so very bad that he's on the verge of screaming, he turns the air-conditioning all the way up and sits there for a while, with the windows rolled up, shivering.

This morning he noticed that the needle had dropped below the half-full mark on the gas indicator, and he told himself that he could put some gas in the car. Just to have something to do. He's trying to insert a five-euro bill into the slot of the self-service gas pump, but because he's had the bill in his pocket for days, it's dirty and wrinkled, and the dispenser keeps spitting it back out. Behind him, a young Chinese man is waiting his turn—let me make this clear, the setting of the nightmare is never in my city, the city is always nondescript, but the young man is always Chinese. He hasn't opened his mouth, he hasn't uttered a sound, but Fabio knows that there's someone behind him, waiting, and it starts to get on his nerves. He loathes having to wait himself, and he loathes the idea of making someone else wait.

Above all, he loathes the idea that the person waiting might take him for an idiot, but the slot keeps spitting out the five-euro note, and so Fabio heaves a sigh and turns around, explaining that it's the dispenser's fault, not his.

He turns around, and he sees that the person waiting behind him is Chinese. He's a young man, possibly the same age as his daughters. He's not looking at Fabio; he doesn't seem to be impatient. He's wearing a jacket with a fur collar that looks like it must have cost a fair amount of money, and he's holding his wallet open and at the ready. Fabio can't help peeking, and he sees plenty of hundred-euro bills, all clean, and one of those rare light-yellow two-hundred-euro bills, and even a five-hundred-euro bill.

Fabio takes a deep breath, turns back to the self-service

pump, and once again the slot spits out his five-euro note. Fabio curses under his breath, and he feels a wave of shame at having only that one banknote to insert into the dispenser, that one and no other. He curses again, in a slightly louder voice this time, passionately. He gives it one more try, and the dispenser spits it out again, only this time the bill slips through his fingers and falls, turning and spinning, wrinkled and filthy, until it lands on the young Chinese man's shiny new shoes.

Fabio leans down to pick it up, but as he curves his back he feels a slight stab of pain, and he instinctively bends his knees to pull himself erect again, but he loses his balance, and in order to keep from falling he's forced to plant one knee and one hand on the ground, and when he's finally able to lay his fingers on the banknote they brush the smooth, shiny leather of the young Chinese man's shoes—and at that very moment *it seems to him that he's just bowed down before him.*

He looks around, but even though no one seems to be looking at him, he feels as if he's just bowed down, and it's simply too much to take, the fact that he's bowed down. He's not a man who bends his knee to anyone, he's never done that. He tells himself that at age fifty, after a lifetime of hard work, he shouldn't have to bow before anyone. He tells himself that if he hadn't been laid off he'd never have felt like this. He feels shame, and he hopes that no one he knows has seen him bow down before a Chinese man.

Because, he thinks, *it was the Chinese who took my job from me*. It's not true. That young Chinese man in particular never stole anyone's job. He's a student, he's attending university, he speaks perfect Italian. He was three years old when he came to Italy. He went to the same school as Claudia, Fabio's younger daughter. They were never in the same classes, but they were in the same grade. If Claudia were there with her father, she'd recognize the young Chinese man. She probably wouldn't say hello to him, or maybe she would, but she'd certainly remember him. She'd know who he was.

For that matter, the father of the Chinese boy, who also lives in the same city as Fabio—which, let me repeat again, isn't my city, but an imaginary city—didn't steal his job, either. The father of the Chinese boy, like nearly all the Chinese who live in that city, does difficult and apparently endless work, at a superhuman pace, work that doesn't know the meaning of breaks and doesn't allow the luxury of memory. It's a kind of work that can be identified with life itself, work that fills life and transcends it. It's a discipline and a duty, a form of dance and a form of torture. It's a self-commissioned theft of everything that makes life worth living. Perhaps it's not even a job, and in any case it certainly has nothing to do with the job that Fabio lost.

Now, the Chinese who are still in China—well, it might be fair to say of them that they *stole* Fabio's job, if we can describe as theft the guiding principle of our impoverished world, its new quintessence, that is to say, the exaltation and the absolute protection of the mobility of employment, our unanimous consensus that jobs should be allowed to cross all borders freely to move wherever labor is cheapest, without breaking any country's laws.

The young Chinese man, like all young men his age, is almost invariably distracted, and rightly so, and he hadn't even noticed the little problem Fabio was having with the automatic gas pump, and only now does he realize, suddenly, that a man is kneeling in front of him, touching his shoes, and so he moves reflexively, out of astonishment and fear, and lifts his foot, and when he puts it down again he steps on Fabio's hand. Unintentionally, of course, and not very hard, because the instant he realizes that he's stepping on Fabio's hand he immediately pulls his foot away—but still he did step on his hand. Not even the whole hand. One finger. He steps on Fabio's pinkie finger. Fabio shouts in pain and shame and surprise, shouts "Fuck you!" and stands up and shoves the young Chinese man hard, with both hands, in the middle of his chest.

He catches the young Chinese man, who's named Zhu, off guard. Zhu slips on one of those treacherous, slippery, half-invisible patches of diesel fuel that often infest the uneven pavement of gas stations, and he falls down. Now Zhu's all dirty. He's sitting on the pavement and looking around, and everyone's staring at him: Fabio, the station attendant, the drivers of the cars lined up to use the gas pumps.

Fabio shouts "Fuck you!" at him one more time, while squeezing his hand, shaking it as if he were an animated cartoon character. For an instant, it's a comical scene, and it wouldn't take much, maybe just a smile, to put an end to it right then and there. But a few seconds go by and no one smiles, and Fabio really is in pain. He tells himself that he might even have broken his finger, and the mere thought that he might have to wade into the hellish bedlam of the emergency room and wait there for hours until someone can put his hand in a cast and then spend a month with the cast on his hand all on account of this idiot Chinese boy, well, right then and there he flips out and starts yelling.

"Goddamned shitty Chinese bastard, to hell with whoever brought you here," he shouts.

He steps closer as if to hit the young man seated on the ground again, filled with an energy he didn't know he possessed, propelled by a wind of rage and impotence that had been gathering within him for years now. He takes two steps, and for a moment he feels better. He feels real, he feels free. Free to be who he really is: not the laid-off man, not the desperate job seeker, not the homunculus driving aimlessly around town with the air conditioner turned up to max. He feels like the man he thought he could become, back when he was twenty.

Anyone watching Fabio would assume he was about to kick the young Chinese man sprawled out on the pavement. That's what I'd think, that's what you'd think too. But Fabio has no intention of kicking him. He's not a violent man, he never has been. All he wants is to emerge victorious from this encounter. He wants to shout "Fuck you!" right in his face one more time, right in the face of this spoiled overgrown Chinese kid with a wallet full of cash, sprawled on the ground, motionless, terrified of him. He just wants to enjoy that last instant of power and then get back in his car, start the engine, and drive triumphantly out of the gas station. It would be his first victory in such a long time.

Zhu, on the other hand, thinks he's being attacked suddenly, for no reason, by an Italian racist. He's twenty-two years old, and even though he's been told over and over again since he was a child to avoid all skirmishes and conflict with Italians, that he simply has to pretend he can't hear the insults and can't see the HANG ALL THE CHINESE graffiti on the walls; that the thing to do is let the knife-sharp glares simply slide off his back, that in practical terms the best thing to do is simply pretend that the Italians don't exist at all, but still, the blood is pumping in his veins the way it does in any twenty-two-year-old anywhere in the world, and he can't put up with being treated like that, he can't allow himself to be kicked when he's down—so he leaps to his feet with the blinding speed unique to young men and delivers a mighty punch to Fabio's face. It's a haymaker typical of the dilettante fighter he is, thrown with eyes closed and hands wide open, one of those punches that never touches the opponent because they're just too slow, but Fabio simply wasn't expecting it and does nothing to block it, and in any case, he wouldn't even know how to block it, and he feels no pain, just a mighty smack to his nose, like when you walk into a sliding glass door or a plate glass wall, and he staggers and falls over backward, and as he falls he hits his head against the sharp corner of the automatic dispenser that just kept spitting out his filthy five-euro banknote, and he loses consciousness and doesn't even realize that his nose and his head are both bleeding, and he lies there with his cheek pressed into the pavement filthy with diesel fuel. He doesn't notice a thing. He just lies there motionless.

There's a terribly long pause. No one says or does anything for several endless seconds, and then one of the motorists waiting in line to fill his tank, let's call him Cassuto, opens his door and gets out of his car and strides vigorously toward Zhu, who stands there frozen to the spot, petrified, open-mouthed in astonishment, at the sight of Fabio crumpled on the pavement. Cassuto yells at him in an incomprehensible dialect, and Zhu turns around to look at him, uncomprehending. When he's six feet away, Cassuto suddenly lowers his voice and mutters, "You filthy piece-of-shit Chinese bastard, so you like to beat up old men, do you?"

And without a moment's hesitation, in a single motion that years of brutal yet unavailing training have carved into his memory, though still without managing to make a professional boxer of him, Cassuto throws a short, venomous right hook at Zhu's face, catching him square on the jaw and shattering it, because Zhu was still standing there open-mouthed in astonishment at the sight of Fabio collapsing on the ground at his feet. It's unbelievable that Zhu manages to remain standing after that punch, and it's also too bad for him, because it gives Cassuto the chance to let fly with a murderous left cross, delivered with every muscle in his shoulders, after which Zhu crumples to the pavement unconscious, limp as a bathrobe.

In line behind Cassuto's car is a van full of Chinese bricklayers, and they see the scene and, shouting in their incomprehensible language, they get out and pile onto Cassuto, and one of them has a hammer in his hand, and another one has a chisel, and so on, and so on, and so on . . .

That's it, that's the nightmare. It goes on from there with protest marches and vigilante groups and broken plate glass windows and clubs and chains and knives, and burning houses and hatred. And madness.

Let me say it again: this is not my city.

But this is the nightmare.

Sistema Italia

Who can say whether there was ever a moment, an hour, a day when we reached the apex of our economic lives and, from that day forth, our dreams became chimeras, our successes privileges, our future an imaginary quantity? Who can say whether it's possible to point a finger and indicate a date we can remember and tell our sons and daughters about, saying that this was the day when everything that had always run smoothly suddenly started to go wrong?

Still, I can try.

It's just a matter of rummaging through one's memories.

During the 1990s, right before China became a member nation of the WTO and its products were allowed to flood the markets of the West like a raging river in spate, our politicians traveled the world with smiles on their faces signing agreements that would ultimately undermine Italy's prosperity, with the enthusiastic support of our economists, who approved and encouraged, repeating in every interview the same childish dogma that the total liberalization of trade would bring the world—the *whole* world, without distinction—much greater advantages than disadvantages.

They said that world and European and Italian consumers would save lots of money with globalization, because the prices of such consumer goods as apparel, computers, washing machines, television sets, DVD players, and a thousand other things—made in China and imported freely without tariffs or customs duties or quotas—would drop, dizzyingly.

They said that the opening of the Chinese market would be doubly advantageous to us Italians, because as soon as they emerged from poverty and had a few yuan in their pockets, what's the first thing the Chinese would rush to buy? But of course, Italian style: our products, the best of the best of world styling and taste, as we could see from the proliferation of Ferrari dealerships and Italian designer boutiques in China, full-fledged bridgeheads for the future landing of the entire Italian national industry in what would soon become the largest and most significant market on earth!

They said that nothing could restrain countless tens of thousands of Chinese, now enjoying a purchasing power that had unexpectedly increased several hundredfold, from running, intoxicated with desire, into a Ferrari dealership to buy a Scaglietti or a Fiorano or a California, which they would drive with a pair of Tod's shoes on their feet, attired in a Giorgio Armani shirt, and wrapped in a pair of comfortable Dolce & Gabbana trousers, and after just a few years the Chinese experience of this incomparable excellence would blaze the paths for Italian style in every walk of life: from fabrics to ceramic tiles, from furniture to bathroom facilities, from shoes to salamis, and so, spearheaded by the best companies, the Italian invasion of the largest, richest market on earth would duly get under way.

We would make piles of money, we Italians, all of us, actually, all of *Sistema Italia*—and if we wanted to speed things up all we had to do was travel to China immediately and open factories there ourselves, both to produce our miraculous products at a much lower cost, blessed by the Made in Italy label, and in order to ready ourselves to start selling over there, in the market of the future, to those 1.5 billion people eagerly awaiting us.

These optimistic tall tales were nothing more than the corollaries of the beautiful fables that every day, for years, the newspapers, the television, and the radio have been telling us, according to which the world had now been settled,

explained, resolved, *one world*: the world of U2's Bono, a dysto-
pian nightmare in which the differences between people and
states—the sacrosanct, iron-bound historical, economic, cultural, religious, and linguistic differences between people and
countries thousands of miles apart, the progeny of completely
distinct histories and cultures—would first be blunted and
later disintegrate into a golden utopia in which all the world's
inhabitants would become citizens of a single empire, sedated
by advertising and led by the nose by television, perfect customers for the paradise of multinational corporations because
they have been indoctrinated into the same tastes, consumers
delighted to eat the same flavorless hamburger wherever they
go, to watch the same storyless movies and listen to the same
plastic music, to spend their days chatting about nothing on
the Internet and never to read a single book, to don the same
pallid imitation of fashion, and all to speak the same language but without having anything left to say at all. A world
in which when you buy a book on Amazon it's shipped to you
airmail from post office boxes 91–93 at the Auckland Mail
Center in Auckland, *New Zealand*, which is to say, the most
expensive way, from the farthest possible place from Italy;
a world in which the Co-op in Prato sells amberjacks, fish
bred and raised *in Australia*; a world giddy with certainties and
definitions, launched headlong toward decadence the way a
beheaded chicken gallops heedlessly; a world that lives at the
antipodes of wisdom and utilizes decades-old technologies

and evidently dismisses as a trifle the cost of transporting things—because without a doubt Amazon and the Co-op may save money by sending me books from New Zealand and selling me Australian tropical amberjacks—and stubbornly insists on overlooking in the price of oil the devastating effects that it has on the planet and on people, and on the future of the planet and on the future of people.

A world governed by the dogmas and the intellectual arrogance of economists, who on a daily basis set out to predict the future like so many shamans, or gurus, or prophets (and still, incredibly, continue to do so). Like seers, card readers, people possessed. Like sorcerers and wizards and haruspices, these gentleman *were predicting the future*, evidently ignorant of the age-old lesson imparted by Francesco Guicciardini, from Renaissance Florence: he warned that *de' futuri contingenti non v'è scienza* (there is no way to foretell the details of the future).

And, of course, they were wrong.

Because things didn't go the way they said they would: the Chinese didn't rush out to buy Italian style, they hurried out and *produced it themselves*, and with the first unmistakable creaks of our industrial manufacturing system (which, until the collapse of borders between the world's markets, represented approximately 50 percent of the entire Italian industrial sector), when a few observers timidly began to point out the sharp rise in bankruptcies and layoffs, the economists furrowed their brows and said that maybe there were still a few Luddites in circulation who hadn't yet read the memo about how we all now live in a single global market; that it was time to wake up and smell the coffee and stop once and for all doing what the Chinese do better; that it was time to increase quality of production and find a place for ourselves in the *specialized market niches*. They told us to go out and do what Enzo Ferrari had done, what Giorgio Armani had done.

Evidently these economists didn't even really know the meaning of *niche*—and that's a shame. Because sometimes knowing the meaning of words can help us to understand reality. According to the Devoto-Oli Italian dictionary, a *niche* is "a hollowed space in a wall, usually in the shape of a vertical semicylinder terminating at the top in a quarter sphere; a decorative element with such a configuration, made especially for a statue, bust, or other ornament." The dictionary goes on, adding that, by extension, the word *niche* has also come to mean "a small repository," that in the jargon of mountain climbers a *niche* is also "a small recess in a rock wall, sufficiently large to shelter a single person," and even though the term is also applied, and properly so, to the field of economics to describe "a specific and circumscribed market area," the Devoto-Oli tells us, basically, that a niche is a den or lair, which can accommodate at most two people, if they really squeeze in. But a country the size of Italy won't fit.

Evidently another thing the economists didn't know was that when you get to China with your lovely assortment of samples, on the very first day, it becomes obvious that you don't have snowball's chance in hell, because the Chinese don't need you or your products—and when it comes to that, the Chinese immediately went into business with the Neapolitans, as Roberto Saviano tells us in such great detail, in his book *Gomorrah*—and they don't need you or your products, which they have long since copied and are currently selling everywhere around the world, including China, for pennies on the dollar.

Evidently the economists didn't know that our small-scale industrialists, manufacturers of fabrics and shoes, bathroom fixtures and household appliances and ceramic tiles and so on, had neither the money nor the lines of credit from banks, nor the ambition nor the luxury, neither the personnel nor the talent, nor the courage nor the recklessness, and neither the vision nor the faith in the future to risk everything they'd built up until that moment, having started out with so little and having been blessed by such great good fortune; that it was ridiculous even to think that an industrial system of small manufacturers could board a plane and move to the opposite side of the planet and shoot up in size over the course of just a few short years, as if there existed some magic yeast capable of causing revenue, bank accounts, workforce, manufacturing structure, business skills, and ambitions to grow miraculously. As if it were random chance that there's only one company in the world called Ferrari. That there's just one, inimitable Giorgio Armani.

No, the economists who were urging small Italian industrialists to move their factories to China really didn't know them at all. They didn't know their history or their work. They didn't take into account that practically all the companies born in the booming postwar years were still being run by their founders, nearly all of whom were about the same age, nearly all of whom were in their sixties or older: a generation of wild enterpreneurs who knew perfectly well that the miraculous growth that their companies had enjoyed was the result of a set of extraordinarily favorable, once-in-a-lifetime conditions, a long and lucky cavalcade on the crest of a wave of epochal growth that sprang from the ruins of postwar Italy and which had lifted everyone, capable and inept, industrialists and employees, well beyond their own limitations.

That their companies had been able to thrive and prosper only in the precious soil where they first sank their roots: shielded from the eye of the tax man and the glare of the law, in a perfect, closed world, protected by barriers and nuclear warheads, by customs policies and tariffs.

That they liked to call themselves industrialists, but they weren't industrialists and never had been.

They were artisans, extraordinary and fragile artisans, the distant great-grandsons of the masters of medieval workshops, and in spite of that they represented the structural framework of an economic system that, incredibly, rested on their shoulders, and even if that system was far from perfect, it worked—and how!—and it was based on what at the time were the rules of the free market. It was a system that had made it possible for Italy to rise from the ruins of a world war, ensured rights and established duties, scattered prosperity and brought employment to millions of people, paid for retirement pensions and hospitalizations, houses and cars, television sets and clothing, created and attained dreams and fostered illusions—and even though the movies and books of those years vied eagerly to mock and scorn it, that chaotic and deeply vital economic system of ours, created by unlettered artisans, was the single most important factor in the transformation of a mediocre, snarling, frightened, Fascist Italy into a modern nation.

This is our story.

The story of millions of people betrayed, in part and primarily, by their politicians, politicians whose only real understanding of the economy was when they were occasionally called upon to administer, depending on who had won an election, either wholesale tax amnesties or haircuts, and meanwhile they were penning hundreds of signatures in complete silence at the bottom of treaties and trade pacts guaranteed to scalp and skin alive the Italian manufacturing industry. Not so much as a referendum, not a strike, not even a demonstration in the streets. Not so much as a law, not a bill or a draft, not even a parliamentary inquiry. Not so much as a hunger strike. Not so much as someone chaining themselves to a pillar in front of Montecitorio, the seat of the Italian parliament. Not even so much as one of those pathetic diatribes on television. Not so much as an appeal, or a petition to save the jobs of those millions of Italians who now find themselves at the mercy of a brand-new, bloodthirsty, roid-raging version of the free market.

Was it a gigantic inferiority complex, whatever it is that prevented and even now continues to prevent our politicians from defending the interests of the Italian manufacturing industry and the millions of people who make their living from it, directly or indirectly? After all, the French politicians defended and continue to defend tooth and nail the subsidies for French agriculture and farmers; the German politicians form a human shield around their extremely powerful chemicals industry; the Swedes and Danes even refused to join the euro for fear of seeing their social welfare state denatured; the British kept the pound sterling and even refused to sign the Schengen Agreement.*

---

* A treaty signed in Luxembourg in 1985, and expanded in 1990, by five of the ten member states of the European Economic Community. It created Europe's Schengen Area, which merges the five member states into one border-free area, with only external border controls for people entering and leaving the area.

So what were our politicians thinking, then, as they signed those sheets of paper in our name and sold our manufacturing industry down the river? Did they really think that there was a way to compete with people who produce the same articles we do at just a fraction of our costs? And how did they think that might be possible? What new products would we have to invent to keep the Chinese from copying them immediately? Perhaps gabardines made with the north wind, flannels made with the crystal-clear water of the river Bisenzio, or lodens made with the olive oil of Filettole? And which new markets would we explore, as urged by our garrulous ministers of foreign trade and economic development—extraterrestrial territories? Venus, shrouded in ammonia clouds? Icy Mars with its rarefied atmosphere? Or perhaps they were thinking of two-faced Mercury, which has one side always turned toward the darkness and the other invariably turned toward the sun, so that we could have sold raw-cut cloth to the Mercurians who live in darkness and grosgrain linen to the Mercurians who live in the sunlight?

Did our politicians know what competition means? Did they know how healthy that term can be? Did they know how much good it can do to a market? But what kind of competition can there be with the economic arm of a dictatorship?

No, we needed to pay lip service to the total opening of international markets while fighting against it in practice. Fighting it from within, of course, without ever mentioning the idea of leaving the euro or Europe, with the proper passion and the proper enthusiasm, the way you have to do every time you're part of an association that starts defending the interests of some members to the detriment of others.

We should have fought tooth and nail, every inch of the way, just as all the other nations did. We should have negotiated, negotiated, and negotiated some more, never tiring of defending our point of view, and we should have sent the really good ones to negotiate—experienced, tough, competent negotiators, the ones who have never read Sun Tzu and don't even know who von Clausewitz was, but who have both those authors' teachings etched onto their hearts and their souls; the ones who instinctively know in the course of a negotiation when the time has come to throw some punches and when, instead, it is necessary to know how to bend like a reed: sons of bitches, in other words, not professors, not those wet rabbits who let themselves be slapped into silence every time they try opening their mouths, mortified and humiliated at the mere mention of that colossal public debt that they have watched swell year in and year out without being able to do anything about it, while at Brussels they continually had it waved in front of their eyes like the scarlet letter of infamy.

It may be easy to say it now that even Romania and Bulgaria have become part of Europe, now that the euro has become the legal currency in Cyprus, Malta, Slovakia, and Slovenia. But I'm convinced that not even the Bundesbank would have had the strength and the interest, in the year 2000, to keep out of the euro by an accounting contrivance (the Maastricht parameters, remember them?)* a country like Italy, one of the founding nations of the United Europe, the cradle of world art, a market with 58 million consumers, an aggressive and rapacious industrial system set in the heart of the Mediterranean basin, willing to devalue the lira anytime it proved convenient and indifferent to the sheer astronomical girth of its public debt, because it had nearly all been financed on the domestic market and was therefore, as time would show, if necessary, perfectly taxable.

We should have been courageous, though, perhaps even reckless. We should have seen how to transform our greatest weakness into strength. We should have read those pages of Machiavelli in which he says that a good prince must "learn something of the nature of localities, and get to find out how the mountains rise, how the valleys open out, how the plains lie, and to understand the nature of rivers and marshes, and in all this to take the greatest care. Which knowledge is useful in two ways. Firstly, he learns to know his country, and is better able to undertake its defense."

We should have abandoned the idea of epic sweep and our gratuitous chest-thumping, and realize that we are the

---

* Parameters stated in the Annex to the Maastricht Treaty: 60 percent for the debt/ GDP ratio and 3 percent for the deficit/GDP ratio.

weakest, the most vulnerable to the cyclone of opening markets, and therefore, in our own interest, take steps to protect ourselves—yes, of course, naturally, *protect ourselves*—with every means possible, from nitpicking to outright brawling, from obstructionism to hugs and kisses, and there was no reason to feel any shame about sending a special trainload of angry thugs to Brussels, now and again, and turning them out into the streets with protest banners to make all their anger heard, and putting our consciences at rest if they happened to break a few windows in buildings occupied by powerful bankers or if one of them happened to get a taste of a Belgian billy club, because it was all for a good cause.

Then, of course, we'd have eventually hauled down the flag all the same. Like the Luddites, we'd have admitted defeat, but we might have won better terms of surrender, and we'd be better off now, and we'd live in a different Italy.

Because, as even our most prominent citizens must fully understand by this point, enthusiastic supporters though they may have been of this damned campaign of laissez-faire globalization, the money that we may save today by purchasing Chinese products is the same money that once paid the salaries of Italian factory workers, the mortgages on their apartments, the monthly payments of their pensions, for their hospital stays, the schools their children attended, their cars, and their clothing.

Their lives, our lives.

Lost

At the end of the film *The Verdict* there's a pearl.

Shafts of light from a setting January sun cut through the motionless air of a Boston courtroom, throwing the shadows of the audience against the dark wooden walls. You hear the judge's voice:

"Mr. Galvin? . . ."

It's a very wide shot. You can see the whole courtroom: the audience, the lawyers, the jury. In the exact middle of the screen is Frank Galvin, an alcoholic lawyer played masterfully by Paul Newman, who remains motionless and says nothing. His hair is graying, his suit is dark, and he stares straight ahead into the void, head bowed. The judge calls him again: "Mr. Galvin, summation? . . ."

Paul Newman remains absolutely motionless for twenty-five seconds, seated, a sheet of paper in his hands, the center-point and immobile fulcrum of the shot, surrounded by other actors and extras who are also motionless. That's an eternity in a movie. It's only after a few seconds that we lose our anxiety to follow the story and we take the time to *watch*. To notice that the shot given to us by the director, the great Sidney Lumet, is beginning to resemble—in the colors, the leaden light, and the immobility—a painting by Rembrandt. To appreciate the void of action and speech that is one of the finest gifts a movie can give us, because it reminds us of all the pauses in our lives. All the time we spend hesitating, doing nothing, saying nothing.

When Paul Newman finally emerges from his immobility it's only to heave a weary sigh. He gets to his feet and prepares to deliver the desperate summation of that fated trial, perhaps his very last. He looks up at the judge—Paul Newman's eyes, which you see glitter even in that very wide shot, so wide it's known in the film business as an *extreme wide shot*—and he begins with a formidable phrase that, believe you me, has nothing to do with the movie that we've seen up to this point and, instead, has a great deal to do with me and with you.

It's the pearl I was promising you.

Paul Newman says: "You know, so much of the time we're lost."

He hesitates for a moment, surprised by the power and the simple truth of what he has just said, and then he goes on with his summation—which is a fine speech, a fervent appeal to the natural sense of justice that, he believes, springs eternal in the jurors' hearts and that in fact allows him to win the case triumphantly and against all expectations— but it's that first, startling phrase that continues to make an impression on me, to move me deeply every time I hear him utter it in that movie that led me so ruinously to choose law back in university, twenty-seven long years ago.

I saw it again last night, *The Verdict*, for the hundredth time. I stumbled upon it as I was surfing the outlying dish satellite channels in search of bloodthirsty documentaries on the way animals live, and I couldn't tear myself away until the very end. I stayed up till three, and this morning I'm exhausted, but the memory of the emotions it stirred is still strong with me as I walk across a Piazza Mercatale full of shy, awkward demonstrators who, like me, give the clear impression they've never been to a protest march before. High above us, the pale February sky seems to be mixed with the clouds until it turns into a soft, endless gray fabric.

It's February 28, 2009, and I'm demonstrating in the street for the first time in my life. For some time now it had been announced that today in Piazza Mercatale there would be a demonstration in support of the Prato textile industry, with the ecumenical participation of all the economic and

political forces of the city. From city hall to the industrialists, to the trade unions and the artisans, from the provin-
cial government to the retailers, from the majority to the
opposition, to the Catholic diocese, they had all urged the
citizenry to come together in one of the largest piazzas in
all of Italy, to count and be counted and escort through
the streets of the city a tricolor streamer so long that it de-
serves to wind up in the *Guinness Book of World Records*. Oddly
enough, the demonstration has a watchword, perhaps even a
title: DON'T SHUT PRATO DOWN.

I came down here with Sergio Vari, my Bolognese friend
who created the writers' fabrics with me for the Lanificio
T.O. Nesi & Figli, the cashmere-Communist bon vivant
who claims that he was in Goa with Led Zeppelin in 1964,
and when you point out to him that in 1964 Led Zeppelin
wasn't a band yet, he replies indignantly that he was with
Robert Plant in Goa in 1964, and just to quit busting his balls
for five minutes.

At demonstrations, as far as I can tell, not a lot gets
done. People talk with other people they know, they listen
to what the others have to say, they walk, they greet people,
they look around. That's all. It must be the most elementary
embodiment of the mechanism of representation, this gathering in the form of mere presences, without any need to say
or shout or even think anything, because my beliefs and my
words are unmistakably represented by the simple fact that

I'm here on the piazza and not at home, not eating lunch with Carlotta and the children. So today what counts is one's body: its extension to become a thought, its ambition to stand in for even those who aren't or couldn't be there.

A concert stage has been set up right in the middle of Piazza Mercatale, and on it city politicians are speaking in stentorian voices—no one came from the national government in Rome—alternating curiously with a large group of singers from La Spezia who perform, one after another, all the saddest songs by Fabrizio De André, so that rather than a protest march it seemed as if we were attending a particularly gloomy wake.

There's not a policeman in sight, not a carabiniere either. No one could imagine problems with civil disobedience from a demonstration organized by people who had done nothing all their lives but work: a single town traffic cop wanders alertly through the piazza with the quick short steps of a jackal, as if he were hungrily asking himself where all these people could have parked their cars.

There's no sign of the *Guinness Book of World Records* streamer. Renato Cecchi, the oldest and the most powerful of all the industrialists of Prato, is on the far side of the piazza from the stage, holding a banner showing the coat of arms of the big fabric-finishing company Santo Stefano, which is big as an airport and clean as an operating room. He looks like a totem, Renato, his hair white as polyester and the sparkling eyes of a little boy, and lots of people come up and greet him, complimenting him on his presence at the demonstration, and then they leave him there, alone, erect as a soldier, holding his banner high.

There are plenty of businessmen among the demonstrators. Some of the older ones are dressed as Pratese industrialists, in those suits made of superfine wool gabardine that only those who have spent much of their lives working on wool and in wool and around wool are likely to choose. But among the younger businessmen quite a few have chosen to camouflage themselves by dressing in suede jackets and jeans, and they slip into every knot of demonstrators and nod as they listen to everyone else's views, both deeply respected and awkward, embarrassed, pleased to be recognized as the bosses even there in the piazza, instantly forgiven for having shown up at the wheel of a Porsche. A little bit they smile and for the most part they nod, surprised and refreshed, enthused at an idea that is so new to them, that Prato is no longer what it has always been, that is, a galaxy of small businesses that are all fervently individualistic, each one facing the world and the harsh dictates of fate alone, but instead a true *economic community* capable of pulling together and speaking in a single voice, even if only for a single day. From the back-slapping and the subdued festive glee that's spreading through the crowd, their relief is unmistakable as they find themselves celebrating a truce, surrounded by others who tomorrow morning will return to being their adversaries, true enough, but who are their friends today, united in the need to fight the same battle against the same enemy, in an all-too-modern latter-day version of the leagues of Tuscan communes that banded together against the invaders that, now and again, descended from the high Apennines or marched up the Arno River valley.

There are a few blue-collar workers and a few students, and just one Chinese protester, the businessman Xu Lin, who just a few days ago was badly beaten by certain compatriots of his with Mafia connections, and he still bears on his face the terrible marks of that beating. Most of the demonstrators are artisans, small and very small businessmen, the category that's been hit hardest by the downturn. It was they who placed in the middle of the piazza dozens and dozens of those plastic crates that are used to ship and store yarn; it was they who arranged them to spell out the watchword of this demonstration: DON'T SHUT PRATO DOWN.

People who didn't know about the display nudged their neighbors and asked what all those crates apparently scattered at random in the middle of Piazza Mercatale were for, because if you didn't know what was happening and you stumbled upon them, in all their bright colors, some of them emblazoned with the names of companies that had long ago gone out of business, they might seem like one of the thousand harlequinades churned out by the overambitious contemporary art that the Italian provinces seem destined to have to put up with for all time.

I look at them for a long time, those crates of yarn, and to my eyes they become an invocation, a supplication that can be seen only from the sky, and even though I know it was all done specifically to allow a helicopter to fly over and take aerial photographs of the demonstration, there is no way to keep from thinking that those crates and that slogan actually also represent a tacit, despairing, powerful prayer to God, since nobody seems to be interested in listening to the voice of my city as it protests.

Because, of course, we're asking the Berlusconi administration to devote to us at least some small part of the attention and money it's budgeting to other economic entities that have been hit by the downturn, entities that are perhaps better known but nonetheless much smaller in terms of turnover and number of jobs than the Prato textile industry, such as Alitalia or even Fiat. In particular, we're asking at least for new financing for the special state subsidy fund on behalf of the many workers who have lost their jobs in recent years, and the huge number after September 2008. Still, it's hard to identify a target this protest is trying to speak to, a guilty party, a bad guy who would be anything other than the status quo of the world, and I find sublime—and unheard of, and proud in its vain ambition—this pragmatic, understated protest on the part of thousands of people who live in the same city but are otherwise separated by everything in life, against the *very essence of things*, against intangible and yet very powerful ideas that are accepted virtually everywhere outside of our city walls, more or less as if we were protesting against the firmament itself, demanding a brighter, more luminous replacement, or against the winter cold.

There's no anger in Piazza Mercatale. You don't see it carved into the faces and you don't hear it quivering in the voice of anyone there. There's bewilderment. There's chagrin. There's a razor-sharp, cursed fear of the future, true enough, but what seems to prevail in everyone's mood is the warm comfort of seeing everyone gather together in a piazza, and so, when an embarassed silence descends after the initial hellos, we immediately give in to nostalgia and start exchanging memories of happier times.

It seems like the right thing to do, under this gray Kieferesque sky that suggests we resign ourselves and tell ourselves that history always finds its own way to bring death to human endeavors, from the greatest to the smallest, and if the empire of Alexander the Great fell, then certainly Prato and the Italy of this tiny, short-lived business empire of ours can fall all too easily, crushed to death in the battle against all odds, the battle against a mistaken idea, mistaken but supported by the *whole world*.

And yet, without a doubt, we should be angry.

Because we've been betrayed. Betrayed by our leading citizens.

Even Mario Monti, a few days ago, wrote an editorial on the front page of the *Corriere della Sera* in which he claimed that "the coordination of public policies, which have in some cases become genuine community policies, has made it possible to govern the opening of the national markets while encouraging growth and without causing excessive turmoil."

I have to confess that I have almost never agreed with the positions held by this president of Bocconi University, but I have always admired the style and the clarity of his statements and, in particular, that fantastic multimillion-euro fine levied against Microsoft, and I wish Professor Monti could be here, right now, in Piazza Mercatale, to see and touch with his hand the dignity of all these people, whose lives and livelihoods have been turned upside down by nothing other than the opening of the national markets, people who have only the vaguest and fondest of memories of the very concept of economic growth.

I'd like to be able to tell Professor Monti that, even if it's written in our future that we're all destined to become economically irrelevant, still I and my family and my city and so many other cities of the Italian provinces where thousands of small businesses sprang up and prospered and provided jobs for hundreds of thousands of people all across the country simply cannot accept in silence that our decline and our sufferings should first be forgotten and then quite simply denied, crossed out with the stroke of a pen—"the most beautiful history in the world . . . the history of me and of my people"—to use the words of the master Fitzgerald, overlooked as if it didn't exist, as if it had never existed.

Because my people are not only the people of Prato.

Among the textile districts that are declining and suffering today are also Biella, Como, Lecco, Carpi, the Val Seriana, Chieri in Piedmont, and Bronte in Sicily; the apparel districts of San Marco dei Cavoti and San Giuseppe Vesuviano; the district of Airola near Benevento and the one in Calitri, also in Campania; the district of Vibrata in Abruzzo and the jeans district of Montefeltro. In Isernia, the largest garment manufacturer producing Italian style, ITR, has gone bankrupt. A crisis is also affecting the ceramics sector in Civita Castellana and Deruta and Sassuolo and Caltagirone and Santo Stefano di Camastra. A similar crisis is afflicting the arms industry of Brescia and lighting systems of the Veneto. There's a crisis in furniture production in Matera and Pesaro and Manzano in Friuli. Also in crisis are the goldsmiths of Arezzo and Valenza Po and Vicenza, as is the eyeglasses district in Belluno. Everywhere, the footwear industry is suffering, in Lucca and Fermo and Vigevano and Santa Croce sull'Arno and Barletta and Castrano.

There's even a crisis in the legendary Brianza.

These are my people, Professor Monti. My people who, in all their lives, have never done anything but work. We are *millions*, and you'll forgive me if I draw you into this book of grief, into this desperate battle that may strike you as a rearguard action, but it is absolutely necessary that from now on you remember us when you talk about community policies with the most powerful people on earth, or it won't take me two minutes to send Tacabanda and his boys to come see you in Milan, and to shake the gates of Bocconi University.

We Can't Take It Anymore

I hear my name being called, and in an instant the thread of my thoughts is torn, and my fury subsides. It's Rolando, a classmate from middle school I haven't seen in years. Shy and taciturn, in our school days Rolando was short, but tough and powerful as a bullwhip, and although he choked up when the teacher was testing him and he could never seem to speak without the heavy accent and the gloomy expression of the peasant that he was, during phys ed he made up for it because in the gym he would show off by grabbing two of those Swedish bars, turning head over heels and, one pole in each hand, hauling himself up by the sheer power of his arms to the ceiling, like a latter-day Hercules, his face bright purple from the effort and his legs straight out in front of him. After middle school, he went to work, first with his father, selecting rags, and later he set up his own weaving mill.

His name isn't really Rolando, but he doesn't want to be identified in this book, so I've given him the name of one of my heroes, Rolando from *La Chanson de Roland*. I see him break away from a small knot of protesters and walk in my direction. He's just a little hunched over, but he looks good for his age. His hair is thick, full, and graying, just like mine. We shake hands, and as he holds me prisoner in the vise grip of his powerful fingers, he turns toward the other protesters and says: "This here is Nesi, the writer. He predicted everything, with that gold book of his."

From the knot of demonstrators, three men look at me without a word. Each of them is carrying a sign. On the first sign is written: WE'RE MUCH BETTER THAN FIAT; on the second, in dialect: WE CAN'T TAKE IT ANYMORE; on the third: WE'RE MADE IN ITALY, TOO.

"Ciao Nesi, we know each other, my grandpa worked as a weaver for your grandpa, and I was a weaver at your company," one of them says to me, the one with the MADE IN ITALY sign, though he doesn't look familiar to me. I shake hands with them, I say *Buon giorno*, and I tell myself that I'm too cold and formal, always too cold with these people, even though I like them and I've always liked them. Why?

"So what do you say about it, Nesi? Whose fault is it? How's it going to end? Are we all really going out of business?" Rolando asks me, looking at me intently, as if he expected a serious answer. I look at him, and I really don't know what to say. I don't feel like getting out of answering with a flip response, not now that the other three men from the small knot of demonstrators have set down their signs and walked over to hear what I think about things. It strikes me as necessary to respond sincerely to their straightforward question, but still I can't bring myself to tell them that it's our fault, too, that we thought we could go on indefinitely doing the same work our fathers did as if it were an established and inviolable right, that we were kidding ourselves if we thought that we could go on in the third millennium selling the same fabrics they used to produce, made out of the same raw materials and the same yarns, weaving them on the same looms, dying them the same colors, finishing them the way our fathers had finished them, selling them to the usual customers in the usual markets.

I look at him without speaking for a good thirty seconds, and then Sergio Vari appears at my side, steers me away by one arm, and tells me that the *strissione*—the streamer—is here and we should go see it. He's right, from the side of a truck they're finally starting to unfurl the much-discussed tricolor streamer that people say is more than a kilometer long, but it's obvious, even from a distance, that there's been a mistake. This isn't a streamer—it looks more like a banner, an infinite banner. Or perhaps it's a standard, an immense standard of hope, to judge from the vast number of people crowding around it, trying to touch it and escort it around the city.

I want to touch it too, and I draw closer. It's made of Prato-manufactured fabric, of course, because all fabrics are Prato-made, and at a glance it looks to me like a *malfilé* cotton, and a pretty nice one at that. I touch it. It has a good, full finish, typical of sportswear. On the white field of the tricolor, repeated dozens of times, the slogan DON'T SHUT PRATO DOWN appears in a dark checked pattern, in the tartan that in Prato we've always called *scozzese*—Italian for "Scotch"—and it's difficult to explain the depth of emotion and heartbreak that suddenly sweeps over me, because the blankets that the Lanificio Nesi made at the beginning were *scozzesi*—a Scotch tartan—before Temistocle and Omero felt they were ready to produce proper fabrics; the shirts I wore every day when I was eighteen had a Scotch check, and I put them on to feel more American; and there was a Scotch pattern on the machine-washable wool flannel that I developed for Ralph Lauren, taking my inspiration from a shirt I saw Kurt Cobain wear in a music video, twenty years ago now, when I was trying to become a businessman.

I move away suddenly, as if I've been burnt, in thrall to sudden memories that I can't believe cause such sharp pain, and I stop to look at the protest streamer that emerges from the belly of the large truck and begins to unfurl across the piazza. I wonder what it must be like to carry it, the infinite banner. It's a part of life that I don't undersand and I've never managed to get into: the communitarian side, in which you participate with other people in things and you are unafraid of setting aside your differences and sharing feelings, opinions, sentiments. I don't know if I'm going to carry it myself. I don't expect I will.

I spot another old classmate I haven't seen in years, Alessandro Sanesi. He breaks off from the procession and comes toward me, he says hello, he grabs me by the arm, and he tells me that when he read *L'età dell'oro* he cried, really cried, and as he says it he looks me in the eye and grips my right arm hard, and it seems as if he's on the point of saying something more, becoming emotional perhaps, and so am I, to tell the truth, because in his presence, thanks to him, I discover how harsh it can be to write about real life instead of making up stories; how it can slowly carve into you and make you crumble apart the way water does with cement and stone; how desperately true it is that a novel can be so much more than a book and become so real that it torments you every day, your characters transfigured into flesh and blood and faces and bodies and voices and infinite banners, and you wind up being held hostage by ghosts that will never let you go because they belong to you. They were created by *you*. They *are* you.

I feel like saying all this to Sanesi, but I can't, because if I do say it I'll only make things worse. If I tell him then it will *become true*, I'll have to tell Carlotta, too, and my father, so I just look at him and say nothing, I shake hands with him, I thank him, and he smiles and thanks me for having written it, that book.

"Really, Edoardo," he says, "thanks a lot."

Then he bids me farewell and heads back to the procession of protesters, and in the blink of an eye he's already vanishing into the distance, and I feel as lonely as I've ever felt in my life, amidst all these people, in this immense piazza. Maybe I should climb onto the stage and silence the La Spezia singers and grab the microphone and ask everyone forgiveness for having written that damned book, and then go home, embrace my children and Carlotta and ask their forgiveness as well and buy the company back and go back to being a textiles manufacturer, and let happen what may, because *I didn't want this*. I didn't want it to end this way, and God only knows how much happier I would have been to be writing about the successes and excesses of my city; how much better suited I would be to recounting the arrogant hijinks of my beloved nouveau-riche compatriots, instead of the tale of their steady decline; how much happier I would have been to be one of them and to have read hundreds of books without having written even one, instead of being a damned 215-pound Cassandra.

The procession sort of swerves to one side, and now here's the streamer coming straight at me, as if it were presenting itself to me, offering itself up. I take a few hesitant steps and I grab it tight, and I immediately feel the immense force of hundreds of people all pushing in the same direction, and I have to start walking along with them, or else the streamer will be torn out of my hands. I have to follow it and carry it at the same time, as if it were a baby, and I hope I have on my face the same embarrassed and yet serene smile as all the other people who are smiling and walking across the piazza with us, holding the hems of this infinite banner that says over and over a hundred times not to shut Prato down. I'm ashamed and yet I tell myself that I did the right thing by coming down here and I couldn't have missed it, that I'm bearing witness, that this is important, and I realize that there are many people waving to me and smiling to see me carrying the streamer. They're almost all men my age, many of them down here with their wives and children, and they don't strike me as sad in the slightest, by no means depressed, by no means defeated as they escort our banner.

Weren't we supposed to be Generation X, after all? Weren't we people without ideas and without ideals, a herd of selfish, lucky assholes, who grew up watching TV, who lived our lives without even noticing how lucky we were, masters of a world where history had been abolished, languidly luxuriating in a golden endless present-day created by the hard work of our fathers?

But isn't there anyone that owes us an apology for having condemned us to be the first generation in centuries that's worse off than our parents' generation? For having brought us into the world and built our sacrosanct dreams of prosperity and then having left us penniless and unemployed when the time came to live those dreams? We go on walking, clutching tight our endless tricolor banner, me and my people, all of us smiling, all of us determined, all of us arrayed compact in the face of malicious fortune—and with every step I take I feel a little better. Now I know that I will never again live in the dazzling Fitzgeraldian splendor in which I thought I luxuriated when I was eighteen and my dreams were boundless and the future was a bright generous gift and life was glistening and weightless like silk, and all around me wherever I looked anyone could try to become a businessman and feel they were masters of their fate, even me. I know now that I am a slave to my books and my family, and that my destiny is to go on writing. As long as I'm able.

But today I want to keep walking alongside my people. I'm not sure where we're going, but we're certainly not standing still.

EDOARDO NESI is an Italian writer, filmmaker, and translator. He began his career translating the work of such authors as Bruce Chatwin, Malcolm Lowry, Stephen King, and Quentin Tarantino. He has written six novels, one of which, *L'età dell'oro*, was a finalist for the 2005 Strega Prize and a winner of the Bruno Cavallini Prize. He wrote and directed the film *Fughe da fermo*, based on his novel of the same name, and has translated David Foster Wallace's *Infinite Jest* into Italian. *Story of My People* won the 2011 Strega Prize—the first nonfiction work to win.

ANTONY SHUGAAR's most recent translations include *On Earth as It Is in Heaven* by Davide Enia, *Romanzo Criminale* by Italian judge and playwright Giancarlo De Cataldo, *Not All Bastards Are from Vienna* by Andrea Molesini, and *Resistance Is Futile* by Walter Siti, winner of the 2013 Strega Prize. He is writing a book about translation for the University of Virginia Press.